The BISQUICK COOKBOOK

Recipes from Betty Crocker in answer to your requests

ILLUSTRATED BY ROGER BRADFIELD

LOREN PAUL HERDER, ART DIRECTOR

Dear Friend,

This is the cook book you helped to write!

Every day, letters pour into our mailbox from homemakers all across the country and even around the world, asking for more and more good Bisquick recipes. Here is some of the wonderful mail you send us, together with the best of the recipes it has inspired.

You'll find good foods a-plenty for all your family meals; extra-quick "convenience" ideas for beginning cooks; company treats and party menus; fine old-fashioned dishes to make the modern way with Bisquick; and even recipes to go with you on vacation to a cabin in the woods or on a camping trip.

Finally, we've shared with you a few of the fascinating adventures with Bisquick that homemakers write to us from faraway places, and our most popular foreign recipes adapted for baking with Bisquick.

We hope you will feel this is really YOUR BISQUICK COOK BOOK—a welcome answer to your questions about easy cooking and satisfying eating at your house, every day in the year.

Cordially,

Betty Crocker

CONTENTS

PAGE

ALL ABOUT
BAKING WITH
BISQUICK

"... I have a little booklet of Bisquick recipes that I enjoy so much. I would like one for my mother if it is available and please let me know if you have a larger Bisquick Cookbook, too"

Mrs Jacob Richter
Ann Arbor, Michigan

Here, in response to thousands of homemakers' requests, we have collected the basic bakings you find on your Bisquick box, together with tips you need for baking success. Read these pages carefully; measure and mix as directed. Then turn to the rest of this little book for hundreds of ways to beautiful baking with Bisquick.

Clip Your Bisquick Bookmark and use it for quick and easy reference with the recipe variations that follow this chapter.

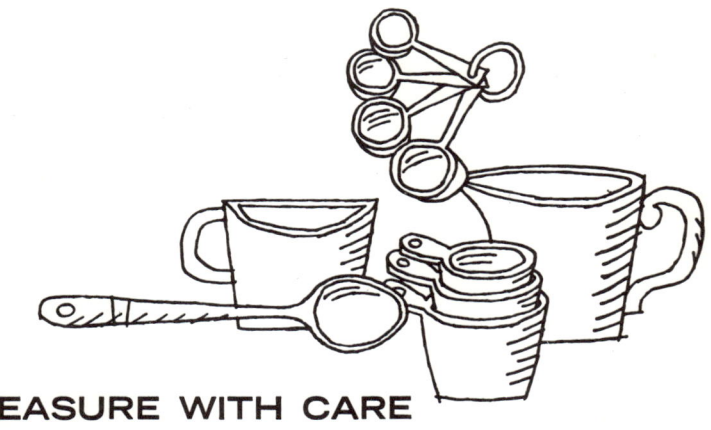

MEASURE WITH CARE

Dry Ingredients

- Never sift Bisquick. To measure, spoon it into dry measuring cup and level surface with knife over waxed paper; pour excess mix back into package.
- Spoon granulated sugar into dry measuring cup and level with knife. Pack brown sugar into dry measuring cup until sugar holds cup shape. Level with knife.
- Spoon confectioners' sugar lightly into dry measuring cup and level with knife. If necessary to remove lumps, press sugar through a sieve.
- Never tap or strike measuring cup. This causes dry ingredients to settle giving overweight.

Soft Shortening

- Be sure shortening is at room temperature. Pack firmly into dry measuring cup or spoon and level with knife.

Liquid Ingredients

- Place liquid measuring cup on level table or counter top. Then pour for exact measurement.
- If non-fat dry milk is used in place of fresh milk, measure after water has been added as directed on package.

<small>My</small> BISQUICK BOOKMARK

BASIC BAKINGS

Biscuits page 7

 2 cups Bisquick
 ⅔ cup milk

Heat oven to 450°. Mix ingredients with fork. Beat vigorously 20 strokes, until stiff and slightly sticky. Knead 8 to 10 times on lightly floured cloth-covered board. Roll ½″ thick. Dip cutter in flour; cut biscuits. Bake on ungreased baking sheet *10 to 15 min. Makes twelve 2″ biscuits.*

½ Recipe: 1 cup Bisquick, ⅓ cup milk.

Pancakes page 8

 2 cups Bisquick
 1 egg
 1⅔ cups milk

Beat with rotary beater until smooth. Grease griddle, if necessary. Turn pancakes when bubbles appear and before they break. *Makes about eighteen 4″ pancakes.*

Waffles page 9

 2 cups Bisquick
 1 egg
 1⅔ cups milk
 2 tbsp. vegetable oil or melted shortening

Beat with rotary beater until smooth. Bake. *Makes three 9″ waffles.*

Shortcake page 10

 2 cups Bisquick
 ¾ cup cream OR
  ½ cup milk plus
  ¼ cup melted butter
  or margarine
 2 tbsp. sugar, if desired

Heat oven to 450°. Mix ingredients with fork. Beat vigorously 20 strokes. Knead 8 to 10 times on lightly floured cloth-covered board. Roll dough ½″ thick. Cut with floured 3″ cutter. Bake on ungreased baking sheet *about 10 min. Makes 6 shortcakes.*

½ Recipe: 1 cup Bisquick, ¼ cup plus 2 tbsp. cream OR ¼ cup milk plus 2 tbsp. butter, 1 tbsp. sugar.

Velvet Crumb Cake
page 11

1⅓ cups Bisquick
¾ cup sugar
3 tbsp. soft butter or
   shortening
1 egg
¾ cup milk
1 tsp. vanilla

Heat oven to 350°. Grease and flour an 8x8x2″ sq. pan. Mix Bisquick and sugar. Add shortening, egg, ¼ cup of the milk. Beat 1 min. at medium speed on electric mixer or vigorously by hand. Stir in gradually the remaining milk and vanilla. Beat ½ min. more. Pour into prepared pan. Bake *35 to 40 min.*

Coffee Cake page 12

2 cups Bisquick
2 tbsp. sugar
¾ cup milk
1 egg

Heat oven to 400°. Mix ingredients. Beat vigorously with spoon ½ min. Spread in greased 9x1½″ round layer pan. Sprinkle with Streusel Topping (p.12) or other topping variation. Bake *20 to 25 min.* For a *Richer Coffee Cake:* add 2 tbsp. more sugar and 2 tbsp. soft shortening.

Muffins page 13

2 cups Bisquick
2 tbsp. sugar
¾ cup milk
1 egg

Heat oven to 400°. Mix ingredients. Beat vigorously with spoon ½ min. Fill greased medium-sized muffin cups ⅔ full. Bake *15 min. Makes 12 muffins.* For *Richer Muffins:* add 2 tbsp. more sugar and 2 tbsp. soft shortening.

Dumplings page 14

2 cups Bisquick
¾ cup milk

Mix well with fork. Spoon onto boiling stew. Cook over low heat 10 min. uncovered and 10 min. covered *Makes 10 to 12 dumplings.*

½ Recipe: 1 cup Bisquick, ¼ cup plus 2 tbsp. milk

Short Pie page 15

1 cup Bisquick
¼ cup butter or
   margarine
3 tbsp. boiling water

Heat oven to 450°. Place Bisquick and butter in bowl. Add boiling water and stir vigorously with fork until dough forms a ball and cleans the bowl. Dough will be puffy and soft. With fingers and heel of hand, pat evenly into a 9″ pie pan, bringing up dough to edge of pan. Flute edges. Bake *8 to 10 min.*

• • • • CUT ALONG DOTTED LINE • • • •

BASIC RECIPE FOR
Biscuits

2 CUPS BISQUICK

⅔ CUP MILK

Heat oven to 450°. Add milk to Bisquick all at once; stir with fork into a soft dough. Beat dough vigorously 20 strokes, until stiff and slightly sticky. Roll dough around on cloth-covered board lightly dusted with flour to prevent sticking. Knead gently 8 to 10 times to smooth up dough. Roll ½″ thick. Dip cutter in flour; cut biscuits. Bake on ungreased shiny baking sheet 10 to 15 min. Makes twelve 2″ biscuits.

½ Biscuit Recipe: 1 cup Bisquick • ⅓ cup milk

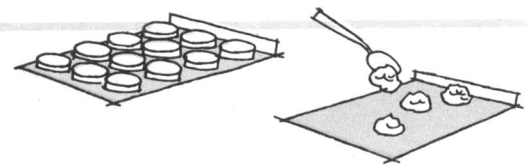

Be sure to heat oven to 450° before mixing biscuit dough. Many a good biscuit never had a chance to rise because the oven was not properly heated. Biscuits made with Bisquick double in volume as they bake.

TIME SAVERS: *Make Drop Biscuits by dropping dough with spoon onto greased baking sheet or into greased muffin cups. Or pat out dough on greased baking sheet; cut with sharp knife into squares or diamonds. Bake as above.*

SEE "BISCUITS" IN THE INDEX FOR VARIATIONS OF THIS BASIC RECIPE.

BASIC RECIPE FOR
Pancakes

2 CUPS BISQUICK

1 EGG

1⅔ CUPS MILK

Beat ingredients together with rotary beater until smooth. Grease griddle, if necessary. Turn pancakes when bubbles appear and before they break. Makes about eighteen 4″ pancakes. For thinner pancakes, add more milk; for thicker pancakes, add more Bisquick.

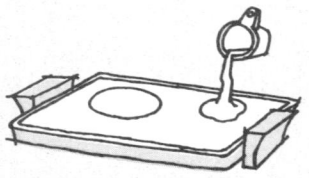

When a few drops of water sprinkled on the griddle "skitter" around, the temperature is right for baking.

To make uniform pancakes of average size, dip the batter onto the griddle with ¼ cup measuring cup.

SEE "PANCAKES" IN THE INDEX FOR VARIATIONS OF THIS BASIC RECIPE.

BASIC RECIPE FOR
Waffles

2 CUPS BISQUICK

1 EGG

1⅔ CUPS MILK

**2 TBSP. VEGETABLE OIL OR
MELTED SHORTENING**

Beat ingredients together with rotary beater
until smooth. Bake. Makes three 9″ waffles.
For crisper waffles, add more milk; for softer,
cushiony waffles, add more Bisquick.

*Pour batter from cup or pitcher into center of hot waffle iron. Avoid
keeping iron open longer than necessary.*

Bake until steaming stops. Lift off the waffle carefully with a fork.

TO FREEZE WAFFLES: *Wrap in foil with waxed paper between waffles
or stack waffles in rigid container with waxed paper between layers.
Reheat by placing in single layer on baking sheet in 400° oven for
5 min., turning once, or reheat in toaster at lowest heat.*

SEE "WAFFLES" IN THE INDEX FOR VARIATIONS OF THIS BASIC RECIPE.

BASIC RECIPE FOR
Shortcake

2 CUPS BISQUICK

3/4 CUP CREAM OR 1/2 CUP MILK
PLUS 1/4 CUP MELTED BUTTER
OR MARGARINE

2 TBSP. SUGAR, IF DESIRED

Heat oven to 450°. Mix ingredients with a fork to a soft dough. Beat vigorously 20 strokes. Knead 8 to 10 times on cloth-covered board, lightly dusted with flour to prevent sticking. Roll dough 1/2" thick. Cut with floured 3" cutter. Bake on ungreased baking sheet about 10 min., or until nicely browned. Makes 6 shortcakes.

1/2 Shortcake Recipe: 1 cup Bisquick • 1/4 cup + 2 tbsp. cream OR 1/4 cup milk + 2 tbsp. butter • 1 tbsp. sugar

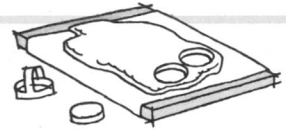

To serve, split shortcakes crosswise while warm. Spread with butter, if desired. Spoon sweetened fruit between layers and over top. Serve with cream, sweetened whipped cream or commercial sour cream.

For a large shortcake, spread the dough in an ungreased 8 x 1 1/2" round layer pan. Bake 15 to 20 min., or until nicely browned. Serve as above.

SEE "SHORTCAKE" IN THE INDEX FOR VARIATIONS OF THIS BASIC RECIPE.

Velvet Crumb Cake

1⅓ CUPS BISQUICK

¾ CUP SUGAR

3 TBSP. SOFT BUTTER OR SHORTENING

1 EGG

¾ CUP MILK

1 TSP. VANILLA

Heat oven to 350°. Grease and flour an 8 x 8 x 2" sq. or 9 x 1½" round layer pan. Mix Bisquick and sugar. Add butter, egg, ¼ cup of the milk. Beat 1 min. at medium speed on electric mixer or vigorously by hand. Stir in gradually the remaining milk and vanilla. Beat ½ min. more. Pour into prepared pan. Bake 35 to 40 min. Serve with Broiled Topping (below) or with other topping, if desired.

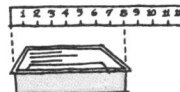 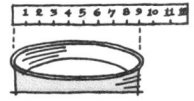

BROILED TOPPING: *Mix 3 tbsp. soft butter, ⅓ cup brown sugar, 2 tbsp. cream, ½ cup coconut, ¼ cup chopped nuts. Spread on baked cake while it is still warm. Place about 3" under broiler until nicely browned, about 3 min.*

Be sure to use the proper size pan as directed in each Velvet Crumb recipe or variation; batter will overflow too small a pan.

SEE "VELVET CRUMB CAKE" IN THE INDEX FOR VARIATIONS OF THIS BASIC RECIPE.

BASIC RECIPE FOR
Coffee Cake

2 CUPS BISQUICK

2 TBSP. SUGAR

¾ CUP MILK

1 EGG

Heat oven to 400°. Mix ingredients. Beat vigorously with spoon ½ min. Spread in greased 9 x 1½" round layer pan. Sprinkle with Streusel Topping (below) or other topping variation. Bake 20 to 25 min. Serve warm and with butter, if desired. For a Richer Coffee Cake: add 2 tbsp. more sugar and 2 tbsp. soft shortening.

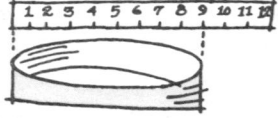

STREUSEL TOPPING: *Sprinkle with mixture of ⅓ cup brown sugar, ⅓ cup Bisquick, ¼ cup cold butter or margarine, ½ tsp. cinnamon, blended with fork until crumbly.*

While coffee cake tastes best fresh from the oven, it may be made ahead and cooled in the pan. Cover with foil to reheat at serving time.

SEE "COFFEE CAKE" IN THE INDEX FOR VARIATIONS OF THIS BASIC RECIPE.

Muffins

2 CUPS BISQUICK

2 TBSP. SUGAR

¾ CUP MILK

1 EGG

Heat oven to 400°. Mix ingredients. Beat vigorously with spoon ½ min. Fill greased medium-sized muffin cups ⅔ full. Bake 15 min. Makes 12 muffins. For Richer Muffins, add 2 tbsp. more sugar and 2 tbsp. soft shortening.

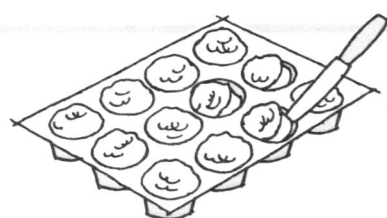

When muffins are done, serve at once or loosen and tip them slightly in cups to prevent sogginess; place in low oven until serving time.

Muffins may be baked in ungreased paper-lined muffin cups.

To reheat leftover muffins, wrap in foil and place in 400° oven 5 to 10 min. or split, butter and toast under the broiler.

SEE "MUFFINS" IN THE INDEX FOR VARIATIONS OF THIS BASIC RECIPE.

BASIC RECIPE FOR
Dumplings

2 CUPS BISQUICK

¾ CUP MILK

Mix thoroughly with fork. Drop by spoonfuls onto boiling stew. Cook uncovered over low heat 10 min. Then cover and continue cooking 10 min. longer. Liquid should just bubble gently. Makes 10 to 12 dumplings.

½ Dumpling Recipe: 1 cup Bisquick • ¼ cup + 2 tbsp. milk

Stew should be boiling when dumplings are dropped; the steam helps them to rise. Drop dough onto meat or vegetables, not into liquid, to avoid absorption of moisture from stew.

To drop dumpling dough easily: Dip spoon into broth each time before spooning dough. Use rubber scraper to slide dough from spoon.

SEE "DUMPLINGS" IN THE INDEX FOR VARIATIONS OF THIS BASIC RECIPE.

BASIC RECIPE FOR
Short Pie

1 CUP BISQUICK

**¼ CUP BUTTER
OR MARGARINE**

3 TBSP. BOILING WATER

Heat oven to 450°. Place Bisquick and butter in bowl. Add boiling water and stir vigorously with a fork until dough forms a ball and cleans the bowl. Dough will be puffy and soft. With fingers and heel of hand, pat evenly into a 9″ pie pan, bringing up dough to edge of pan. This may seem skimpy but will not be when baked. Flute edges. Bake 8 to 10 min.

This makes a soft, rich, cooky-like crust, an excellent base for highly flavored foods. Use for pie shells, tarts and meat pies.

Flour hands lightly to prevent dough from sticking to fingers.

Pat out dough evenly to insure uniform browning.

SEE "SHORT PIE" IN THE INDEX FOR VARIATIONS OF THIS BASIC RECIPE.

FAMILY'S
CHOICE

"I almost couldn't cook without Bisquick, which I always use in gravies* as well as for muffins and shortcake, all of which my family requests frequently.

Mrs. Johanna Brewer
Davis, California

I think Bisquick is a lifesaver ... I enjoy using it and hearing the praises of my cooking from family and friends.

Mrs. Irene Kaminski
Warren, Michigan

Letters like these from homemakers all across America tell us that Bisquick is busily at work in their kitchens helping to prepare their families' favorite foods for every meal of the day. Blueberry pancakes for breakfast, meat pie for lunch, hot rolls for dinner—what is *your* family's choice? These recipes—some new, many tried-and-true—will guide you as you go, sunup to sundown, happily baking with Bisquick.

*See page 42 for Good Brown Pan Gravy

Breakfast Brighteners, p. 19/Lunch or Suppertime, p. 27/Dinner is Served, p.41.

17

Pancakes Plain and Fancy, p. 19; with Sausage Ball Syrup, Maple Whip and Lemon Syrup, p.

Nut Waffles, p. 21; Chiffon Waffles with Cherry Sauce, p. 21; Date Muffins, p. 23.

Buttons and Bowknots, p. 25; Orange Polka Dot Coffee Cake, p. 23; Jolly Breakfast Ring, p.2

BREAKFAST BRIGHTENERS

PANCAKES PLAIN AND FANCY

Make Pancakes from Basic Recipe (p. 8).
Then try all these delightful variations.

Apple Pancakes

Add 2 cups grated unpeeled apples, 2 tbsp. sugar and 1 tbsp. lemon juice to batter. Bake. Serve hot with Cinnamon Maple Syrup (p. 22).

Banana Pancakes

Add 1 cup mashed ripe bananas (2 med.), 1 tbsp. lemon juice and 2 tbsp. sugar to batter. Bake. Serve with honey or currant jelly.

Blueberry Pancakes
(See picture opposite)

Add 2 tbsp. sugar to batter; gently fold in 1 cup fresh or drained canned blueberries. Bake. Serve dusted with confectioners' sugar.

Blueberry Spice Pancakes

Add 1 tsp. cinnamon, 1/2 tsp. nutmeg and 1/4 tsp. cloves to batter. Spoon onto griddle; sprinkle drained blueberries, fresh, frozen or canned on top. Bake. Serve with Lemon Syrup (p. 22).

Cranberry Pancakes

Use only 1 1/2 cups milk and fold 1/2 cup canned cranberry sauce into batter. Bake. Serve warm with remaining cranberry sauce heated with 2 tbsp. light corn syrup.

Orange-Nut Pancakes

Fold grated rind of 1 orange and 1/3 cup pecans (finely chopped) into batter. Bake. Serve with heated maple-flavored syrup.

Prune-Nut Pancakes

Add 1/2 cup chopped uncooked prunes, 1/2 cup chopped nuts and 1/2 tsp. ginger to batter. Bake. Serve hot with your favorite syrup.

Sesame Seed Pancakes

After pouring batter on griddle, sprinkle each pancake immediately with 1 or 2 tsp. toasted sesame seeds*. Bake. Serve hot with Orange-Maple Syrup. (p. 22).

Toasted Coconut Pancakes

Fold 1 cup toasted coconut** into batter. Bake. Serve with heated maple-flavored syrup. Sprinkle more toasted coconut over top.

• • •

To toast sesame seeds, place on flat pan or baking sheet in 400° oven 5 to 10 min. Stir occasionally with fork.

• • •

**To toast shredded coconut, spread loosely on flat pan or baking sheet. Place in 350° oven 10 to 15 min. until nicely browned. Stir occasionally with fork.*

EARLY BIRD SUMMER BREAKFAST

Cantaloupe Wedges
Blueberry Spice Pancakes
with Lemon Syrup (left)
Broiled Canadian Bacon
Coffee and Milk

PANCAKES CHILDREN LOVE

Lanky Doodle Pancakes

Long, long pancakes—a novelty that appeals to children. Grownups think they're fun, too!

Make batter from Basic Pancake Recipe (p. 8). Pour ⅓ cup batter to form an oblong pancake instead of a round one. Bake. *Makes about 12 long pancakes.*

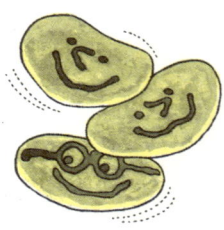

Smile Cakes

Start the day with a smile! First bake the face and then the cake.

Make batter from Basic Pancake Recipe (p. 8). In a cup combine 4 tsp. batter with 1 tsp. maple-flavored syrup. To form eyes, mouth, etc., let this mixture trickle from teaspoon onto hot griddle. (Space the design within a 3″ area.) When brown on bottom, do not turn but pour about ½ cup regular batter over the face and bake. Serve one Smile Cake on top of stack of 3 or 4 plain pancakes.

Silver Dollar Pancakes
(See picture, p. 18)

Make batter from Basic Pancake Recipe (p. 8). Spoon one tablespoonful at a time to fill griddle with tiny pancakes. Bake. *Makes about 60 small pancakes. 4 to 6 servings.*

Animal Pancakes

Bake up a pancake menagerie!

Make batter from Basic Pancake Recipe (p. 8). Form simple animal designs on pancake griddle by pouring batter for round pancake; then with a spoon, add small amounts of batter to represent ears, tail, feet, etc. Bake.

Butterfly Pancakes

Bake pancakes from Basic Recipe (p. 8). To serve, cut pancakes through center. Place curved sides together to resemble a butterfly. Place a sausage in center of body.

Jack-O'-Lantern Pancake Stack

A Halloween morning surprise!

Bake pancakes from Basic Recipe (p. 8). Stack several pancakes on serving plate. Cut eyes and mouth out of top pancake to resemble a jack-o'-lantern. Place 2 small sausage pieces in eyes; a triangle of butter for the nose; several sausage links for hair.

WONDERFUL WAFFLES

Golden-crisp and tender—once a special Sunday breakfast treat, now so easy you can make them for every day. Mix the batter in a pitcher; set it by the waffle iron—invite everyone to pour and bake his own.

Make Waffles from Basic Recipe (p. 9).
Then try all these delicious variations.

Bacon Waffles
Lay short strips of bacon over grids of heated waffle iron. Close and bake about 1 min. Pour batter over cooked bacon and bake. Serve with syrup.

Nut Waffles
(See picture, p. 18)
Add ¾ cup finely chopped pecans, peanuts or walnuts to batter. Bake. Serve with Maple-Apricot Syrup (p. 22).

Spicy Waffles
Add 1 tsp. cinnamon, ½ tsp. allspice, ½ tsp. cloves and ½ tsp. nutmeg to batter. Bake. Serve with sweetened applesauce.

Blueberry Waffles
Add 2 tbsp. sugar to batter. Gently fold in 1 cup fresh or drained canned blueberries. Bake. Serve with confectioners' sugar.

Banana Waffles
Add 1 cup mashed ripe bananas (2 med.), 1 tbsp. lemon juice and 2 tbsp. sugar to batter. Bake. Serve with currant jelly or dust with confectioners' sugar.

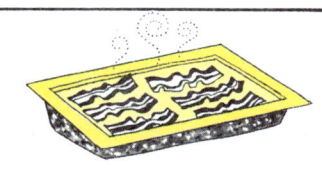

**BREAKFAST MEAT
IN MINUTES**

Bake bacon or pork sausages in 400° (mod. hot) oven. More can be done at one time, there's no need to watch, and the top of the range is free for other things. Bacon takes 10 min., pork sausages 20 to 30 min., turning once.

Chiffon Waffles
(See picture, p. 18)
High, light and handsome—delicate "puff" waffles.

    2 eggs
    1 cup milk
    2⅓ cups Bisquick
    2 tbsp. sugar
    ¼ cup vegetable oil or
        melted shortening

Beat eggs with rotary beater until soft peaks form. Blend in milk. Add Bisquick and sugar. Mix just until thoroughly dampened. Fold in oil. Spoon onto heated waffle iron. Bake until steaming stops and waffles are a golden brown. Serve hot with Cherry Sauce. Makes three 9″ waffles.

SPECIAL SYRUPS
FOR PANCAKES AND WAFFLES

Maple Rum-Flavored Syrup

Heat 1 cup maple-flavored syrup with 1 tbsp. butter or margarine. Remove from heat; stir in ½ to 1 tsp. rum flavoring. Serve warm.

Maple-Apricot Syrup

Heat ¾ cup maple-flavored syrup with 1 tbsp. butter or margarine and ¼ cup apricot nectar. Serve warm.

Maple-Nut Syrup

Heat 1 cup maple-flavored syrup with 1 tbsp. butter or margarine. Remove from heat; blend in ¼ cup chopped pecans or toasted almonds. Serve warm.

Cinnamon-Maple Syrup

Heat 1 cup maple-flavored syrup with 1 tbsp. butter or margarine and ½ tsp. cinnamon. Serve warm.

Orange-Maple Syrup

Heat 1 cup maple-flavored syrup with grated rind of 1 orange and 1 tbsp. butter or margarine. Serve warm.

Maple Whip

Cream ½ cup soft butter or margarine. Add 1 cup maple-flavored syrup gradually. Beat until smooth and spreading consistency. This is marvelous with biscuits and may be refrigerated for future use.

Honey Butter

Beat ½ cup honey with ½ cup soft butter or margarine. Add 1 tsp. grated orange rind; beat until fluffy.

Lemon Syrup

Mix ½ cup sugar, 1 tbsp. cornstarch and ⅛ tsp. salt in saucepan. Gradually stir in 1½ cups hot water. Bring mixture to a boil, stirring constantly. Simmer 5 min. Remove from heat. Blend in 3 tbsp. butter or margarine, 2 tbsp. lemon juice, 1 tsp. grated lemon rind and ½ tsp. nutmeg. Serve warm. *Makes about 1½ cups.*

Sausage Ball Syrup
(See picture, p. 18)

Serve tiny sausage balls swimming in maple-flavored syrup—no need to cook another breakfast meat.

> ½ lb. bulk pork sausage
> 1⅓ cups maple-flavored syrup

Form pork sausage in small balls, ½″ in diameter. Cook thoroughly about 10 min. Drain sausage balls; add to syrup. Heat slowly 5 min. Serve hot over pancakes.

Hawaiian Pineapple Sauce

Mix 1 can (1 lb. 4 oz.) crushed pineapple (2 cups), ¼ cup brown sugar (packed) and 2 tbsp. butter or margarine. Bring to boil; simmer gently about 3 min. To thin topping, add a little water. Serve warm on waffles with broiled ham.

MUFFINS BY THE DOZEN
COFFEE CAKES, TOO

Serve them warm and fragrant—fresh from the oven.

Make Muffins from Basic Recipe (p. 13). Then try all these delicious variations.

Fruit Muffins
(See picture, p. 18)
Use recipe for Richer Muffins. Fold 1 cup fresh berries (or ¾ cup well drained canned berries or 1 cup cut-up dates or figs) carefully into the batter.

Whuffins
Use recipe for Richer Muffins. Fold 1½ cups Wheaties carefully into the batter.

Bacon Muffins
Fold ¼ cup crisp diced cooked bacon into batter.

Oatmeal Muffins
Add ¾ cup oatmeal to batter.

Prune, Apricot or Pineapple Coffee Cake
Make Coffee Cake from Basic Recipe (p. 12). Spread batter into greased 9x9x2″ pan. Top with 2 tbsp. butter or margarine, melted. Sprinkle with ¼ cup granulated or brown sugar and ¾ tsp. cinnamon. Arrange 1 cup chopped, drained cooked prunes or apricots or 1 cup drained crushed pineapple over top. Bake. Serve warm.

LAZY DAY BREAKFAST

Half Chilled Grapefruit with Maraschino Cherry and Juice
Scrambled Eggs and Bacon
Orange Coffee Cake (below)
Coffee and Milk

Orange Coffee Cake
(See picture, p. 18)
There's tangy fresh orange juice right in the batter.

2 cups Bisquick
½ cup sugar
¾ cup orange juice
1 egg
2 tbsp. shortening, melted

Heat oven to 400° (mod. hot). Mix all ingredients. Pour into greased 9x9x2″ pan. Finish with Polka-Dot Orange Topping or Orange Caramel Topping (below). Bake *20 to 25 min.* Serve warm.

Polka-Dot Orange Topping:
Blend 2 tbsp. softened butter or margarine, 2 tbsp. Bisquick, 2 tbsp. brown sugar, ½ tsp. cinnamon and 1 tbsp. grated orange rind. Drop about ¼ tsp. at a time spaced evenly over the top of the batter in pan.

Orange Caramel Topping:
Mix ¼ cup chopped nuts, ½ cup brown sugar, 1 tsp. cinnamon, 2 tbsp. softened butter or margarine and 1 tbsp. grated orange rind. Sprinkle over top of batter in pan.

BEAUTIFUL BISCUITS

So light they fairly float—flaky, crusty, golden-brown, they double in size as they bake. Out of the oven in minutes—delicious for breakfast with butter and honey, jam or jelly.

Make Biscuits from Basic Recipe (p. 7).
Then try these interesting variations.

Jolly Breakfast Biscuit Ring
(See picture, p. 18)
Caramel-crusted and gaily studded with cherries and nuts.

Heat oven to 400° (mod. hot). Shape Biscuit dough into 12 balls. Melt ⅓ cup butter or margarine and pour about 3 tbsp. of it into a 9″ ring mold. Sprinkle with 3 tbsp. brown sugar, 12 cherries (candied or maraschino) and ¼ cup chopped nuts. Roll balls in rest of melted butter, then in mixture of ½ cup sugar, 1 tsp. cinnamon, 3 tbsp. chopped nuts. Place in ring mold. Bake *25 to 30 min.* Take from pan while warm.

Butterscotch Biscuit Rolls
Old-fashioned butterscotch flavor—be sure to serve warm.

Heat oven to 425° (hot). Roll Biscuit dough into rectangle, 16x7″. Spread with 2 tbsp. softened butter or margarine. Sprinkle with a mixture of ¼ cup sugar (granulated or brown) and 1 tsp. cinnamon. Roll up tightly, beginning at wide side. Seal well by pinching edge of dough into roll. Cut into 1″ slices. Place 2 tsp. butter or margarine, melted, 2 tsp. brown sugar and 2 or 3 pecans in each of 16 greased medium-sized muffin cups. Place roll cut side up on top of this mixture. Bake *about 15 min. Makes 16 rolls.*

Pecan Rolls: Add ½ cup chopped pecans to the sugar-cinnamon mixture.

To cut roll into 1″ slices, slide string under roll. Then hold one end with each hand. Next bring ends together at top of roll of dough. Cross ends, pull string tight to cut through dough.

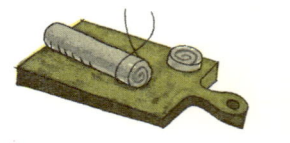

SPECIAL FOR BREAKFAST

Bake up a surprise—wake up sleepy morning appetites.

Buttons and Bowknots
(See picture, p. 18)
Clever little hot breads that taste like doughnuts.

> 2 cups Bisquick
> 2 tbsp. sugar
> 1 tsp. nutmeg
> ⅛ tsp. cinnamon
> ⅔ cup cream OR ½ cup milk
> 1 egg

Heat oven to 400° (mod. hot). Mix Bisquick, sugar, and spices. Add cream, egg; mix well. Dust hands and cloth-covered board lightly with flour. Knead 2 or 3 times. Keep dough soft. Roll out ½" thick. Cut with floured doughnut cutter. Save "holes" to bake. Hold opposite sides of ring with fingers; twist to make figure 8. Pat scraps together, reroll and cut. Place on ungreased baking sheet. Bake *10 to 12 min.*, until golden brown. Melt ¼ cup butter or margarine. Measure ½ cup sugar into small bowl. Immediately after baking, dip each quickly in butter, then in sugar, coating all sides. Serve warm. *Makes about 10.*

Cinnamon Roll
Good, old-fashioned cinnamon rolls—so homey, they're everybody's favorite.

> 1 egg
> 3 cups Bisquick
> ¾ cup milk
> 2 tbsp. softened
>   butter or margarine
> ¼ cup sugar
> 2 tsp. cinnamon

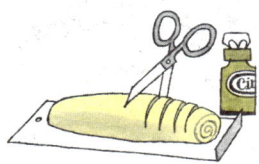

Heat oven to 400° (mod. hot). Beat egg; add Bisquick and milk. Stir to make soft dough. Turn onto lightly floured cloth-covered board. Knead lightly, just until smooth. Pat or roll out into a rectangle, 10x8". Spread with butter. Sprinkle with mixture of sugar and cinnamon. Roll up tightly beginning at wide side. Seal well by pinching edge of dough into roll. Place sealed side down on ungreased baking sheet. Make cuts with scissors almost through roll at intervals of 1". Bake *about 20 min.* While warm, glaze top with mixture of ¼ cup confectioners' sugar and 2 tbsp. warm water. *Makes 10 to 12 slices.*

Monday Meat Pie, p. 33; Tuna Ring with Bleu Cheese Sauce, p. 32; Corned Beef Pinwheels, p. 28

Beaten Hamburger Onion Buns, p. 35; Cheese Twists, p. 36; Tiny Marmalade Biscuits, p. 3

Cranberry Puffs, p. 39; "Gingie" Pudding, p. 37; Strawberry Baskets, p. 38.

FOR LUNCH OR SUPPERTIME

What to do with a pound of hamburger . . .
quick, hot and hearty meat pancakes and pies!

Hamburger Pancake Roll-ups

Served with buttered broccoli.

Make Pancakes from Basic Recipe (p. 8)—except add ⅓ cup more milk. Bake each pancake about 6″ in diameter. Spoon 2 tbsp. Crumbled Hamburger (below) on each pancake. Roll and place folded side down in oblong baking dish, 13x9½x2″. Cover with ½ to 1 cup grated sharp cheese. *Heat thoroughly in 350° (mod.) oven, about 10 min.*

Crumbled Hamburger: Brown 1 lb. ground beef, 2 tbsp. instant minced onion in 2 tbsp. fat. Add 2 tbsp. Bisquick, ⅓ cup catsup, 1 tbsp. prepared mustard, ½ tsp. salt, ¼ tsp. pepper, 1 cup commercial sour cream. Simmer 5 to 10 min.

SUPPER-IN-A-DISH
Topsy Turvy Pie (right)
Spiced Crab Apples
Carrot and Celery Sticks
Velvet Crumb Cake (p. 11)

Topsy-Turvy Pie

Bake, turn upside down and serve in wedges.

 1 lb. ground beef
 2 tbsp. vegetable oil
 ½ cup chopped onion
 ¼ cup chopped green pepper
 1 can (8 oz.) tomato sauce
 ¼ cup water
 1 tsp. salt
 1 tsp. chili powder
 1 can (4½ oz.) chopped
  ripe olives

Heat oven to 425° (hot). Brown meat in oil; add onion and green pepper. Cook, stirring frequently, until meat is well browned and onion is transparent. Add rest of ingredients. Mix well. Pour into 9″ pie pan. Make Topping (below). Roll out to fit top of pie pan. Make slits on top. Place over meat mixture. Bake *15 to 20 min.* Remove from oven. Let stand a minute or two. Invert over serving dish. Cut in wedges. *4 to 6 servings.*

Topping: Mix 1 cup Bisquick and ⅓ cup cream. Beat 20 strokes. Roll dough on cloth-covered board lightly dusted with flour to prevent sticking. Knead 8 to 10 times to smooth up.

CORNED BEEF DISHES

Hasty, tasty ways to use a can of hash!

Corned Beef Biscuit Pinwheels

(See picture, p. 26)

Baked in onion soup for zippy flavor.

    1 can (10½ oz.) onion soup plus
       water to make 2 cups OR
      1 env. dry onion soup plus
      2 cups water
    2 cups Bisquick
    ¾ cup cream
    1 can (15 oz.) corned beef hash
    ¼ tsp. pepper

Heat oven to 450° (hot). Pour soup into 9x9x2″ pan; bring to boil. Blend Bisquick and cream; beat 20 strokes. Turn out onto lightly floured board; knead 6 to 8 times. Roll out into 12x8″ rectangle. Spread corned beef hash over dough; sprinkle with pepper. Roll up like jelly roll. Cut in slices 1½″ thick with a sharp knife. Place in pan containing hot onion soup. Bake *30 min. 4 servings.*

Corned Beef Bake

Serve with a relish tray—carrot sticks, celery and black olives.

    1 can (15 oz.) corned beef hash
    2 tbsp. Bisquick
    1 egg, slightly beaten
    ¼ cup milk
    2 tbsp. chopped onion
    salt and pepper to taste
    ¼ cup catsup
    ½ cup grated cheese
    Short Pie dough

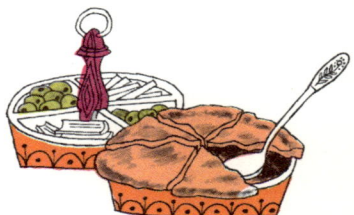

Heat oven to 375° (quick mod.). Grease an 8″ pie pan. Mix all ingredients except Short Pie dough. Pack into pie pan. Make Short Pie dough from Basic Recipe (p. 15). Divide into 6 equal parts. Pat each part into equal sized pie-shaped wedges between hands. Place on top of pie filling, leaving a little opening between each piece for appearance and ease in cutting. Bake *30 to 35 min.,* or until crust is done and deep golden brown. *6 servings.*

HAM AND LUNCHEON MEAT DISHES

Hurry-up Ham Casserole

. . . transforms leftover ham.

    1 can (3 oz.) sliced mushrooms
      (⅔ cup)
    ⅓ cup diced onion
    2 tbsp. butter or margarine
    1 tbsp. flour
    1 can (10½ oz.) cream of
      celery soup
    ½ soup can milk
    2 cups cubed cooked ham
    ½ recipe Biscuit dough

Heat oven to 450° (hot). Brown mushrooms and onion in butter. Add flour; blend well. Dilute cream of celery soup with milk; add with ham to onion-mushroom mixture. Bring to boil, stirring occasionally. Pour into ungreased 1½-qt. baking dish. Make ½ Biscuit dough from Basic Recipe (p. 7). Drop by spoonfuls onto hot mixture. Bake *15 to 20 min.*, or until biscuits are nicely browned. *4 to 6 servings.*

Dixie Bake

Speedy, delicious brunch idea.

    1 can (12 oz.) luncheon meat
    12 whole cloves
    Biscuit dough
    ½ cup apricot jam
    ½ tsp. dry mustard
    1 tbsp. water

Heat oven to 425° (hot). Slice luncheon meat into 12 squares almost through to bottom. Stud with whole cloves. Place in 8x8x2″ baking dish. Make Biscuit dough from Basic Recipe (p. 7). Cut into 12 biscuits. Surround meat with biscuits. Spread meat and biscuits with mixture of jam, mustard and water. Bake *20 min.*, or until biscuits are golden.

Tomato Juice — Sausage and Dumplings

Savory sausage and delicate, pink-tinted dumplings. Serve in a soup bowl with a buttered green vegetable on the side.

    ½ lb. bulk pork sausage
    1 can (1 lb. 2 oz.) tomato
      juice (2¼ cups)
    ½ tsp. salt
    ⅓ cup milk
    1 cup Bisquick

Shape pork sausage into small patties. Brown on both sides in a deep saucepan. Drain off excess fat. Add tomato juice and salt. Heat to boiling. Mix milk and Bisquick thoroughly with a fork. Drop by spoonfuls into boiling juice. Cook over low heat for 10 min. uncovered and 10 min. covered. Liquid should just bubble gently. Remove dumplings; serve with sauce and sausage. *3 to 4 servings.*

CREAMED CHICKEN OR TURKEY DISHES

Chicken Griddle Cakes

Make Pancake batter from Basic Recipe (p. 8). Bake 8 large pancakes (5 to 6" in diameter), using about ½ cup batter for each. Spoon ¼ cup Creamed Chicken (below) onto half of each pancake. Fold over other half. Place on baking sheet. Sprinkle with grated sharp yellow cheese (about 1 tbsp. for each cake). Slip under broiler or in oven for a moment to melt cheese. Serve on warm plates. *8 servings.*

Creamed Chicken

    2 tbsp. butter or margarine
    ¼ cup Bisquick
    ½ tsp. salt
    1½ cups milk
    2 cups finely diced cooked
      chicken
    pepper
    poultry seasoning or
      other herbs

Melt butter. Remove from heat. Blend in Bisquick and salt. Gradually stir in milk. Bring to boil over low heat, stirring constantly. Boil 1 min. Stir in chicken. Season to taste with pepper and poultry seasoning. Heat until chicken is hot.

Chicken Roll-ups

Serve with buttered peas and cranberry sauce for a wonderful luncheon.

Heat oven to 450° (hot). Mix 2 cups chopped cooked chicken with gravy or white sauce to moisten, about ½ cup. Make Biscuit dough from Basic Recipe (p. 7). Roll dough ¼" thick into rectangle, 18x9". Spread with chicken mixture. Roll up, beginning at wide side. Seal well by pinching edge and ends of dough into roll. Cut into slices 1½" thick. (For smooth and easy slicing see (p.24). Arrange slices cut side up in well greased shallow baking pan (close together for roll-ups with soft sides . . . with spaces between for roll-ups with crusty sides). Bake *15 to 20 min.* Serve immediately with gravy or Mushroom Sauce (p. 46). *Makes 12 roll-ups.*

SUNDAY EVENING SUPPER
Chicken Griddle Cakes (left)
Buttered Broccoli
Sliced Tomatoes
Sherbet 1-2-3 Cookies (p. 39)
Coffee   Milk

Turkey may be used in place of chicken in any of these recipes.

SEAFOOD SUPPER DISHES

Unusual "fish day" inspirations.

Deep Dish Salmon-Cheese Pie

Perfect served with lemon sherbet.

1 tbsp. chopped onion
2 tbsp. butter or margarine
¼ cup Bisquick
1½ cups milk
1 cup grated sharp
   Cheddar cheese
1 can (1 lb.) salmon, drained
   and broken in large pieces
1 tsp. salt
few grains pepper
½ recipe Biscuit dough

Heat oven to 450° (hot). Sauté onion in butter. Remove from heat. Blend in Bisquick. Slowly stir in milk. Bring to boil over low heat, stirring constantly. Boil 1 min. Stir in rest of ingredients . . . except Biscuit dough. Turn hot mixture into greased 1½-qt. baking dish; heat in oven until mixture bubbles. Make ½ recipe of Biscuit dough from Basic Recipe (p. 7). Pat or roll to fit top of baking dish. Cut 2 to 3 slits in center. Place on hot mixture. Bake *about 15 min.*, or until biscuit crust is brown. *4 to 6 servings.*

**SEA WORTHY TIPS
ON SERVING FISH**

To enhance fresh fish flavor, sprinkle with a small amount of one of the herbs: basil, dill, oregano, marjoram or rosemary, or serve with lemon butter.

Davy Jones Tuna Bake

Serve with sliced tomatoes.

2 cups Bisquick
1 cup milk
3 eggs
½ tsp. salt
⅛ tsp. pepper
2 cans (7 oz. each) tuna,
   flaked, with oil
½ cup grated sharp cheese
1 tbsp. chopped onion
¼ cup chopped pimiento
⅓ cup chopped celery

Heat oven to 400° (mod. hot). Grease a 9x9x2" or 11x7x1½" baking pan. Blend Bisquick, milk, eggs, salt and pepper. Beat vigorously 30 seconds. Mix in 1½ cans of the tuna, ¼ cup of the cheese, onion, pimiento and celery. Spread batter in prepared pan. Sprinkle the remaining ¼ cup cheese over top. Bake *30 to 35 min.* Serve with Tuna Celery Sauce (below). *8 servings.*

Tuna Celery Sauce: Blend 1 can (10½ oz.) cream of celery soup with 1 cup milk and remaining ½ can tuna. Heat and serve.

TUNA WITH CHEESES
BLEU OR PARMESAN

Ring-Around Tuna with Bleu Cheese Sauce

(See picture, p. 26)

2 cans (7 oz. each) tuna,
　with oil
½ cup chopped onion
½ cup grated sharp cheese
¼ cup chopped parsley
1 tsp. celery salt
½ tsp. salt
¼ tsp. pepper
1 egg, slightly beaten
Biscuit dough

Heat oven to 375° (quick mod.).
Mix tuna, onion, cheese, parsley,
seasonings and all but 2 tbsp. egg.
Make Biscuit dough from Basic
Recipe (p. 7). Roll in rectangle,
15x10″. Spread with tuna mixture.
Roll like jelly roll, starting with wide
side. Place on well greased baking
sheet in ring shape, seam side down.
Pinch ends together. Make 12 cuts
⅔ of the way through the ring at 1″
intervals. Turn each piece on its side
to show filling. Brush with remaining
egg. Bake *25 to 30 min.* Serve with
Bleu Cheese Sauce (below). Garnish
with parsley. *4 to 6 servings.*

Bleu Cheese Sauce: Melt ¼ cup
butter or margarine over low heat.
Blend in ¼ cup Bisquick and ¼
tsp. *each* salt and pepper. Stir over
low heat until smooth and bubbly.
Remove from heat. Stir in 2 cups
milk. Boil 1 min., stirring constantly.
Add ½ cup crumbled Bleu cheese.

Tuna Royal Pancakes

New!! Parmesan-pimiento flavors!

Pancake batter
1 can (7 oz.) tuna, drained
　and flaked
¼ cup chopped onion
½ cup grated Parmesan cheese
½ cup chopped celery
¼ cup chopped pimiento
2 tsp. lemon juice
1 can (10½ oz.) cream of celery
　or chicken soup
2 tbsp. Bisquick
¼ tsp. salt
⅛ tsp. pepper
2 cups milk

Make Pancake batter from Basic
Recipe (p. 8)—except add ⅓ cup
more milk. Bake ten 5″ pancakes.
Keep warm between towels until
ready to serve. *Heat oven to 400°*
(mod. hot). Mix tuna, onion, ¼ cup
of the cheese, celery, pimiento and
lemon juice. Spoon 2 tbsp. of mixture
on each pancake. Roll and place
folded side down in 11x7x1½″ or
9x9x2″ baking pan. Heat in oven
about 10 min. Mix soup, Bisquick,
salt, pepper and milk. Heat until
thickened. Pour over pancakes;
sprinkle with remaining ¼ cup
grated cheese. Place under broiler
until bubbly. *10 servings.*

GIVE A LIFT TO LEFTOVERS

Leftover Meat Roll

Serve in savory slices and pass the sauce boat, please.

>2 cups leftover meat, cut up
>1 small onion, finely chopped
>¼ cup chili sauce
>Biscuit dough

Heat oven to 425° (hot). Mix meat, onion, chili sauce. Make Biscuit dough from Basic Recipe (p. 7). Roll Biscuit dough into a rectangle ½" thick. Spread with meat mixture. Roll up, beginning at wide side. Seal well by pinching edge of dough into roll. Place sealed side down on greased baking sheet. Make several slashes on top to let steam escape. Bake *about 25 min.* Cut into thick slices; serve hot with sauce made by heating 1 can (10½ oz.) tomato soup and ½ cup milk together. *4 servings.*

Ham Roll: Follow recipe above—except use 2 cups flaked or chopped cooked leftover ham moistened with a little white sauce. Serve roll hot with creamed peas, eggs or mushrooms.

Monday Meat Pie

(See picture, p. 26)
What to do with Sunday's roast.

>½ cup diced celery
>½ cup diced onion
>½ cup chopped green pepper
>2 cups cut-up cooked meat
>2 cups cut-up cooked vegetables
>2 cups well seasoned gravy
>½ recipe Biscuit dough

Heat oven to 450° (hot). Brown celery, onion and green pepper in hot fat. Add rest of ingredients . . . except Biscuit dough. Pour mixture into greased 1½ qt. baking dish. Place in oven; heat until mixture bubbles. Make ½ recipe Biscuit dough from Basic Recipe (p. 7). Roll or pat to fit top of baking dish. Cut 2 or 3 slits in center. Place over bubbling mixture. Bake *15 min.* Serve hot. *6 servings.*

BEEFWICH FILLING

Grind leftover beef roast with an onion. Mix with pickle relish and chopped hard-cooked eggs. Add mayonnaise to moisten. Spread on Beaten Hamburger Onion Buns (p. 35).

WHEN YOU WANT TO SERVE "SOMETHING SPECIAL"

Saucy Pigs In Blankets

New flavor excitement—try other sauces, too.

Heat oven to 450° (hot). Make Biscuit dough from Basic Recipe (p. 7). Roll in large circle ⅛" thick. Cut circle in 8 equal wedges. Spread each wedge with 1 tbsp. well drained sauerkraut. Roll a frankfurter in each wedge, starting at wide end; seal well by pinching tip into roll. Sprinkle rolls with poppy seeds. Place on greased baking sheet. Bake *about 15 min.* Serve immediately with hot tomato sauce and additional sauerkraut on the side. *Makes 8 servings.*

Potato Skillet Cakes

Save cold mashed potatoes for this appetizing dish.

- 1 egg, beaten
- 1 cup cold mashed potatoes
- ½ cup milk
- 2 tbsp. vegetable oil or melted shortening
- 2 cups Bisquick

Mix all ingredients; beat with rotary beater until mixture is smooth and thick. Drop by tablespoonfuls onto hot greased griddle or skillet. Bake slowly (about 5 min. on each side). Serve hot with gravy, maple syrup or jelly. *Makes about 25 cakes.*

Meat Cakes: Add ½ to 1 cup chopped cooked meat to the dough.

Fritters

For a change of pace, serve fritters for supper—fruit or corn—with syrup and bacon.

- 2 cups Bisquick
- ⅔ cup milk
- 1 egg
- 2 cups fruit or cooked vegetables (cut-up pineapple, peaches, corn, etc.), drained

Mix Bisquick, milk, egg until well blended. Stir in fruit or vegetables. Drop by small teaspoonfuls into deep hot fat (360 to 375°).* Turn and fry until golden brown on both sides. Drain on absorbent paper. Serve hot with syrup or confectioners' sugar. *Makes about 2 doz.*

*To use a minimum of fat for frying, melt fat in a deep 2 or 3 qt. kettle which is only 7 or 8" wide across the top. Two cups of fat will give a depth of about 1", sufficient for frying.

Rivvels

An old Pennsylvania Dutch recipe . . . heavenly good in homemade vegetable soup.

- 2 eggs
- ⅛ tsp. salt
- ¼ cup water
- 1 cup Bisquick

Beat eggs. Stir in rest of ingredients until smooth. Drop by teaspoonfuls into your favorite vegetable soup. Cook 3 to 5 min.

BUNS, BREADS AND BISCUITS

Your own homemade hamburger buns—really quick and easy, too.

Beaten Hamburger Onion Buns

(See picture, p. 26)

  1 pkg. active dry yeast
  1¼ cups warm water
    (not hot—110 to 115°)
  2 tbsp. sugar
  4 cups Bisquick
  2 tbsp. dried onion flakes

In mixer bowl, dissolve yeast in warm water. Add sugar and half the Bisquick. Beat 2 min. medium speed on mixer or 300 vigorous strokes by hand. Scrape sides and bottom of bowl frequently. Add remaining Bisquick and onion flakes; blend with spoon until smooth. Scrape batter from sides of bowl. Cover with cloth and let rise in warm place (85°) until double, about 30 min. (If kitchen is cool, place dough on a rack over a bowl of hot water and cover completely with a towel.) Stir down by beating 25 strokes. Drop dough by spoonfuls on greased baking sheet making 12 mounds, spacing 2″ apart. Dough will be sticky. Flatten tops with floured fingers in rounds about ½″ thick. Again, let rise in warm place (85°) for 40 min.

Heat oven to 400° (mod. hot). Bake *12 to 15 min.*, or until nicely browned. Brush tops with shortening. Serve warm or cold as hamburger buns.

Cocktail Buns

Follow recipe above—except drop dough by teaspoonfuls on greased baking sheet about 1″ apart. Do not flatten. Bake *10 to 12 min.* Serve warm with ham, turkey, etc. as snack buns. *Makes about 4 doz.*

VARIATIONS

Cheese Buns: Follow recipe (left)—except omit onion flakes. Add ⅓ cup grated sharp cheese and 2 tbsp. finely cut pimiento. Serve with hamburger or ham.

Caraway Buns: Follow recipe (left)—except omit onion flakes; add 2 tbsp. caraway seeds, 1 tsp. crumbled sage and ½ tsp. nutmeg. Serve with sliced chicken or turkey.

Pickle Buns: Follow recipe (left) —except omit onion flakes; add ⅔ cup coarsely chopped candied dill pickles, ½ cup chopped nuts and 2 tbsp. finely cut pimiento. Serve with sliced ham.

To Freeze: Cool; wrap in heavy-duty aluminum foil; freeze. To reheat, do not unwrap but place frozen in 325° (mod.) oven for 20 min.

```
PATIO PICNIC SUPPER
Grilled Hamburgers
on Onion Buns (left)
Potato Salad
Cherry Tomatoes    Dill Pickles
Fudge Squares (p. 84)
Chilled Fruit Beverage
```

A tisket, a tasket . . . take a pretty basket, line it with a napkin and fill with piping hot Muffins (p. 13) or fluffy Biscuits (p. 7). Serve with butter and honey to make a feast of a light supper.

Cheese Twists
(See picture, p. 26)
Good with rich beef stew.

½ recipe Biscuit dough
¼ cup soft butter or margarine
⅓ cup grated American cheese

Heat oven to 450° (hot). Make ½ Biscuit dough from Basic Recipe (p. 7). Roll into rectangle. Spread with butter and cheese. Roll up like a jelly roll; fold ends to center; roll out again ¼″ thick. Cut into narrow strips 5″ long. Twist. Place on greased baking sheet. Sprinkle with salt and paprika. Bake *6 to 8 min.*

Caraway-Cheese Twists:
Sprinkle caraway seed over cheese before rolling up the dough.

Butter Sticks
Golden brown, hot and buttery.

Heat oven to 450° (hot). Melt ⅓ cup butter in oblong pan, 13x9½x2″, in oven. Remove as soon as butter melts. Make Biscuit dough from Basic Recipe (p. 7). Roll into rectangle, 10x6″. Cut in half lengthwise. Cut each half into 12 strips (about 3x½″). Dip each stick in butter; arrange in pan. Bake *10 to 15 min.*

Corn Meal Butter Sticks
Follow directions for making Butter Sticks (above) except sprinkle corn meal over melted butter in pan. Make Biscuit dough from Basic Recipe (p. 7)—except substitute ½ cup corn meal for ½ cup of the Bisquick. Salt lightly before baking. Bake *10 to 15 min.*

Tiny Marmalade Biscuits
(See picture, p. 26)
A sweet trick—bite-sized biscuits.

Heat oven to 425° (hot). Spread ½ cup orange marmalade mixed with 2 tbsp. soft butter or margarine in 8x8x2″ pan. Make Biscuit dough from Basic Recipe (p. 7). Roll into an 8″ sq. Place dough over marmalade-butter mixture. Cut into 36 small squares. Bake *15 to 20 min.* Invert pan on serving plate. Biscuits will break off into small bite-sized pieces. Serve warm.

DESSERT DELIGHTS

End the meal with a perfect pudding . . . warm, spicy, satisfying.

"Gingie" Pudding

(See picture, p. 26)

An unforgettable dessert with unusual and delectable flavors.

⅓ cup butter or margarine
2 tbsp. water
¼ cup molasses
⅓ cup brown sugar (packed)
2 cups Bisquick
½ cup brown sugar (packed)
¼ tsp. ginger
¼ tsp. cloves
1 tsp. cinnamon
½ cup chopped nuts
2 tbsp. soft butter
⅔ cup milk
¼ cup molasses
1 egg

Heat oven to 350° (mod.). Melt butter in 8x8x2″ pan. Add water and and ¼ cup molasses. Sprinkle the ⅓ cup brown sugar evenly over bottom of pan. Mix Bisquick, ½ cup brown sugar, spices and nuts. Stir in butter, milk, ¼ cup molasses and egg until dry ingredients are dampened. Beat 30 seconds. Pour batter over sauce in pan. Bake *40 to 45 min.* Serve warm topped with a dab of softened cream cheese and covered with Fluffy Lemon Sauce (below). *6 to 9 servings.*

Fluffy Lemon Sauce: Mix in saucepan ½ cup sugar, 2 tbsp. cornstarch. Stir in gradually 1 cup boiling water. Boil 1 min., stirring constantly. Remove from heat. Stir in 1 tbsp. butter, ¼ cup lemon juice and 2 tsp. grated lemon rind. Gradually blend into 1 egg, well beaten.

Ranch Pudding

This rich pudding makes its own butterscotch sauce.

1 cup brown sugar (packed)
2½ cups water
2 tbsp. butter or margarine
1 cup brown sugar (packed)
½ cup milk
1¼ cups Bisquick
1 cup raisins or chopped dates
½ to 1 cup chopped nuts
1 tsp. vanilla

Heat oven to 350° (mod.). Mix 1 cup brown sugar, water and butter in saucepan. Boil 5 min. Pour into 8x8x2″ pan. Mix rest of ingredients in bowl. Spoon batter on top of sugar mixture. It will spread as it bakes. Bake *45 min.* Serve warm with either plain or whipped cream. *9 servings.*

SALAD LOVERS' SUPPER
Caesar Salad
Butter Sticks (p. 36)
"Gingie" Pudding (left)
Coffee   Milk

JUICY FRUIT SHORTCAKE STARS IN ANY SEASON

Once-A-Year Shortcake Supper

At the height of the summer season, make a whole meal of crusty-tender golden shortcake, served warm and generously buttered, then heaped with fresh sliced peaches or strawberries. Pass a pitcher of cream or a bowl of sweetened whipped cream, and serve with steaming hot, good coffee! Let your family eat their fill —good enough for company, too.

Strawberry Baskets
(See picture, p. 26)
Shortcakes go sophisticated.

Heat oven to 450° (hot). Make Fruit Shortcake dough from Basic Recipe (p. 10). Roll about ⅛″ thick. Cut in 8 rounds with a 4 or 5″ cutter (or use top of coffee can). Fit rounds over backs of lightly greased custard cups, tart pans or muffin pans. Bake *about 8 min.*, or until evenly browned. Remove from cups immediately.

Wash, hull and cut 1 qt. strawberries into halves. Sweeten with ½ cup brown sugar (packed). Beat 1 pkg. (3 oz.) cream cheese and ¼ cup cream together with fork until fluffy. Spread insides of shortcake baskets with creamed cheese mixture; fill with sweetened berries. Serve immediately. *Makes 8 servings.*

Winter Shortcakes
Who needs fresh fruit? Serve one of these for dessert some snowy day.

Make Shortcake from Basic Recipe (p. 10), and top with one of the following:

Pineapple-Apple-Cranberry Topping: Mix together 1 cup canned crushed pineapple (8½-oz. can), 1 cup finely chopped or grated red-skinned apple (1 med. apple), 1 cup finely chopped fresh cranberries, ¼ cup sugar and ⅛ tsp. salt. Let stand at room temperature ½ to 1 hr. before serving.

Warm Cranberry Sauce: Heat cranberry sauce (canned or homemade).

Canned Fruit: Heat 1 can (1 lb. 13 oz.) fruit, (such as sliced peaches, apricot halves, plums, etc.). Blend in 2 tbsp. cornstarch dissolved in 2 tbsp. cold water. Bring to boil over direct heat, stirring constantly. Boil 1 min. Stir in 2 tbsp. butter until melted. Cool. Serve.

EXTRA!

Tasty tricks with shortcake dough: Add 1 tsp. grated lemon rind OR ¼ cup grated sharp cheese OR ½ tsp. ground cardamom to dough. Bake and **serve** warm with any fruit.

FRESH FROM THE OVEN
CAKE AND COOKIES

Date Velvet Crumb Cake

Tender, fluffy, date-flavored crumb cake—cuts easily warm or cold.

> 1 pkg. (8 oz.) dates, cut up
> (about 1½ cups)
> 1 cup water
> 1½ cups Bisquick
> ¾ cup sugar
> 3 tbsp. soft shortening
> 1 egg
> ⅓ cup milk
> ¼ cup chopped nuts

Heat oven to 350° (mod.). Grease and flour an 8x8x2″ pan. Bring dates and water to rolling boil; boil 1 min., stirring constantly. Set aside while mixing cake. Mix Bisquick and sugar. Add shortening, egg and milk. Beat 1 min. at medium speed on electric mixer or vigorously by hand. Add ¾ cup of the date mixture (save rest for topping); beat ½ min. more. Pour into prepared pan. Bake *35 to 40 min.* Cool slightly before spreading with the remaining date mixture. Sprinkle chopped nuts over top. Serve with whipped cream, if desired.

Velvet Crumb Cupcakes

Heat oven to 400° (mod. hot). Make Velvet Crumb Cake batter from Basic Recipe (p. 11). Pour into medium-sized paper-lined muffin cups. Fill ½ full. Bake *about 15 min.* Remove from paper cups. Serve with whipped cream and well drained crushed pineapple, folded together. *Makes 12 cupcakes.*

Cranberry Puffs

(See picture, p. 26)
Bright-flavored holiday treat.

> ¾ cup chopped cranberries
> ½ cup sugar
> 1 cup Bisquick
> ½ cup sugar
> 1 egg
> ⅓ cup milk

Heat oven to 400° (mod. hot). Mix ½ cup sugar with chopped cranberries. Set aside. Blend rest of ingredients. Beat vigorously 30 seconds. Divide sweetened cranberries evenly among 8 large well greased muffin cups. Add muffin mixture, filling each ⅔ full. Bake *about 15 min.* Serve immediately, inverted, with Butter Sauce (p. 53).

1-2-3 Cookies

Quickest family cookies going.

> 1 cup peanut butter
> ¼ cup soft butter or margarine
> 1 cup granulated sugar OR
>   1 cup brown sugar (packed)
> ½ cup boiling water
> 2 cups Bisquick

Heat oven to 400° (mod. hot). Mix peanut butter, butter, sugar and boiling water. Blend with rotary beater or spoon until smooth. Stir in Bisquick. Drop by teaspoonfuls onto lightly greased baking sheet. Flatten with fork dipped in flour. Bake *8 to 10 min.*, or until set but not hard. *Makes about 6½ doz.*

Oven-Crisp Chicken and Biscuits, p. 44; Country Fried Steak, p. 41: Baked Meat Sandwich, p. 4

Biscuits and Rolls, p. 47; Beaten Raisin Bread, p. 49; Onion Biscuit Squares, p. 48.

Strawberry Glacé Short Pie, p. 50; Mocha Spice Velvet Crumb Cake, p. 52; Pear à la Crème, p. 5

DINNER IS SERVED

MEAT MAIN DISHES

Country Fried Steak
(See picture opposite)
Rich, brown well-seasoned
steak with gravy.

Cut 1 lb. round steak into serving-size pieces. Dip in mixture of ½ cup Bisquick, ½ tsp. salt, ⅛ tsp. pepper and ⅛ tsp. paprika. (Save leftover dipping mixture for gravy.) Brown meat slowly and thoroughly on all sides in a little hot fat. Add small amount of liquid (2 to 3 tbsp.). Add more liquid as needed. Cover tightly and cook over low heat until tender, 1 to 2 hr. For added seasoning, cook meat with sliced onion. *For Gravy:* Remove meat from pan. Add 1 cup water to drippings in pan. Mix 1 to 2 tbsp. of the leftover dipping mixture with ¼ cup water and add slowly to hot liquid, stirring constantly. Bring to a boil; boil 1 min. Season to taste. Add meat and serve. *4 servings.*

```
FATHER'S FAVORITE
DINNER
Country Fried Steak (above)
Mashed Potatoes
Buttered Peas
Relishes
Hot Biscuits (p. 7)
Upside-Down Cake (p. 79)
Coffee     Milk
```

Meat and Vegetable Pie

    1 lb. stewing beef (cubed)
    ½ cup Bisquick
    ½ tsp. salt
    ⅛ tsp. pepper
    ⅛ tsp. paprika, if desired
    1 medium tomato, chopped, OR
      ½ cup canned tomatoes
    1 to 2 small onions, chopped
    2 large carrots, sliced
    1 small clove garlic, cut up
    ½ tsp. Worcestershire sauce
    salt and pepper
    ½ recipe Biscuit dough

Roll meat in mixture of Bisquick, salt, pepper and paprika. Brown meat thoroughly on all sides in a little hot fat. Add tomatoes, onions, carrots and garlic; sauté until onions are transparent. Add enough water to cover meat and vegetables. Cover tightly and cook over low heat until meat is tender, 1½ to 2 hr. Add Worcestershire sauce, salt and pepper.

Heat oven to 425° (hot). Make ½ recipe Biscuit dough from Basic Recipe (p. 7). Pour stew in 1½-qt. baking dish. Top with biscuits; bake *about 12 min.,* until biscuits are a golden brown. *2 to 3 servings.*

For added flavor: Add ¼ cup chopped parsley or cut-up chives to biscuit dough.

LET'S HAVE STEW WITH DUMPLINGS

Lamb Stew with Mint Dumplings

Hearty lamb stew topped with mint dumplings. Delicious!

- 2 lb. boneless lamb shoulder, cut in 2" cubes
- 2 cups hot water
- 2 tsp. salt
- ¼ tsp. pepper
- 1 small bay leaf
- 3 medium carrots, cut in 1" pieces
- 1 medium onion, sliced
- 1 medium potato, diced
- 1 cup fresh or frozen peas
- Dumpling dough
- ½ tsp. dried mint leaves

Brown meat in 2 tbsp. hot fat over medium heat in Dutch oven or deep, heavy skillet. Add water and seasonings. Simmer, covered, 2 hr., adding more water if needed. Add carrots, onion and potato; cook over medium heat 20 min. Add peas. Thicken stew by stirring in 2 tbsp. Bisquick mixed with ¼ cup cold water. Make Dumplings from Basic Recipe (p. 14)—except add ½ tsp. crumbled mint leaves to dough. *6 servings.*

Good, Brown Pan Gravy: For each cup of gravy desired, use 2 tbsp. fat, 2 tbsp. Bisquick and 1 cup liquid. Remove meat from pan and pour off fat into a small bowl. Measure fat back into pan; stir in Bisquick and cook over low heat, stirring constantly until mixture bubbles. Remove pan from heat and stir in liquid. Return pan to heat and stir thoroughly to scrape in the rich drippings. Boil 1 min. Season and serve.

Breaded Veal

- 1½ lb. veal cutlet (or 6 veal chops)
- 1 cup Bisquick
- 1 egg, slightly beaten
- ¼ cup fat or drippings
- ½ cup boiling water
- salt and pepper to taste

Wipe veal with damp cloth and cut into 6 serving-sized pieces. Trim off outer skin and pieces of hard tissue. Dip meat in Bisquick, then in egg and again in Bisquick. Brown meat in fat. Slide spatula under meat to loosen from pan before turning. After browning, add boiling water. Season with salt and pepper. Cover and cook about 45 min., or until meat is tender. Remove cover a few minutes before serving to crisp coating on meat. *6 servings.*

Crispy Fried Liver

Trim skin and membrane from 1 lb. baby beef liver. Leave in serving-sized pieces or cut in strips ¾x4". Dip in Bisquick, then in milk and again in Bisquick. Fry in hot fat over medium heat until crispy brown, about 5 min.; turn and fry on other side. Season with salt and pepper. *4 servings.*

With Bacon: Fry bacon first; remove and keep warm while frying liver.

With Onions: Fry liver; remove and keep warm. Put sliced onion rings in fat; cover and steam until soft. Uncover; cook until golden brown.

WITH FLAVORFUL, TENDER PORK

Savory Pork Pie

Good chop suey flavor . . .
with biscuits added.

    1½ lb. pork butt
    2 tbsp. fat
    tops of 6 celery stalks, chopped
    1 medium onion, diced
    1 tsp. salt
    ⅛ tsp. pepper
    1½ cups boiling water
    ½ cup light cream
    Biscuit dough

Cut pork into 1″ cubes. Dredge well in flour and brown in fat. Add celery, onion, seasonings and water. Cover and simmer 1½ to 2 hr. If needed, add water during cooking period. Add cream; bring to a simmer. Place in 10x6x1½″ oblong or 8x8x2″ sq. baking dish.

Heat oven to 450° (hot). Make Biscuit dough from Basic Recipe (p. 7). Cut with biscuit or doughnut cutter; place on top of hot meat mixture. Bake *10 to 12 min. 6 to 8 servings.*

Note: 1½ tsp. poultry seasoning may be mixed with the Bisquick when making the biscuits.

Baked Meat Sandwich
(See picture, p. 40)

    1 lb. ground lean pork
    ½ cup chopped onion
    ¼ cup grated Parmesan cheese
    ½ cup grated Swiss cheese
    1 egg, beaten
    ¼ tsp. Tabasco
    1½ tsp. salt
    2 tbsp. minced parsley
    Biscuit dough
    ¼ cup mayonnaise
    1 egg yolk

Heat oven to 400° (mod. hot). Cook pork and onion over low heat until no longer pink. (Do not brown. Stir with fork to break up as it cooks.) Cool. Mix in cheese, egg, Tabasco, salt and parsley. Make Biscuit dough from Basic Recipe (p. 7)—except add ¼ cup mayonnaise. Spread half in well greased 8x8x2″ sq. pan. Cover with meat mixture. Spread rest of dough over mixture. (The top will even out during baking.) Brush with beaten egg yolk to give a crusty glaze. Bake *25 to 30 min.* Cut in slices about ½″ wide and serve hot or cold. *4 to 6 servings.*

LICKIN' GOOD CHICKEN AS YOU LIKE IT . . .

Oven-Crisp Chicken and Biscuits
(See picture, p. 40)

    1 cup Bisquick
    2 tsp. salt
    ¼ tsp. pepper
    2 tsp. paprika
    ½ cup shortening (half butter)
    1 frying chicken, cut-up
    Biscuit dough

Heat oven to 425° (hot). Mix Bisquick, salt, pepper and paprika in paper bag. Place shortening in oblong pan, 13x9½x2″, and set in oven to melt. Shake 3 or 4 pieces of chicken at a time in bag to coat thoroughly. Place chicken, skin side down, in single layer in hot shortening. Bake *45 min.;* turn.

Make Biscuit dough from Basic Recipe (p. 7). Roll dough ½″ thick; cut into biscuits. Push chicken to one side in pan; place biscuits in single layer on other side. Bake another 15 min. or until biscuits are lightly browned and chicken is tender.

Place chicken and biscuits on serving platter. For gravy, add 2 tbsp. Bisquick (saved from dredgings) to drippings in pan. Bring to boil. Add about 1½ cups hot water. Boil 1 min. *4 servings.*

Chicken Pot Pie
Rich with chicken-flavored biscuit topping.

    ¼ cup chicken fat, butter or
      margarine
    ¼ cup Bisquick
    1½ tsp. salt
    ¼ tsp. pepper
    2 cups chicken stock (saved
      from stewing chicken)
    ⅔ cup cream
    3 to 4 cups cooked chicken (cut
      in large pieces)
    2 cups Bisquick
    ¼ cup chicken fat
    ½ cup milk

Heat oven to 450° (hot). Heat chicken fat and blend in ¼ cup Bisquick, salt and pepper. Remove from heat; stir in chicken stock, cream and chicken. Cook over low heat until thickened (about 5 min.). Mix vigorously with fork, 2 cups Bisquick, ¼ cup fat and milk. Knead 8 to 10 times on surface lightly dusted with flour. Pat or roll dough to fit top of baking dish, 11x7x1½″ oblong or 9x9x2″. Cut 2 or 3 slits in center of dough. Pour *hot* filling into baking dish. Cover with dough. Bake *about 15 min. 4 to 6 servings.*

Stuffing Balls
A different and delicious accompaniment to chicken or turkey.

Heat oven to 400° (mod. hot). Make Biscuit dough from Basic Recipe (p. 7)—except add 1 tsp. each instant minced onion, dried celery flakes, dried parsley flakes and poultry seasoning. Divide into 12 balls. Roll balls in a mixture of ¼ cup butter or margarine, melted, and 2 cups bread crumbs. Place on baking sheet. Make indentation with spoon in each ball. *Bake 12 to 15 min.* When ready to serve, fill indentation with whole cranberry sauce.

HERE'S DINNER BAKED IN A PIE

Corn and Shrimp Pie

Crispy-crusted party casserole. Just add salad and dessert.

⅓ cup chopped green pepper
2 tbsp. finely chopped onion
2 tbsp. fat
2 tbsp. Bisquick
1 tsp. salt
¼ tsp. pepper
1 can (1 lb.) cream-style corn (about 2 cups)
1 egg, slightly beaten
1½ cups cleaned cooked shrimp (two 5-oz. cans OR 1 pkg. frozen shrimp)
½ recipe Shortcake dough

Heat oven to 450° (hot). Sauté green pepper and onion in hot fat until soft. Blend in Bisquick, salt and pepper. Stir in corn. Stir constantly until mixture comes to a boil. Remove from heat. Stir a little of hot mixture into the egg. Blend into remaining hot mixture. Stir in shrimp. Pour hot mixture into greased 1½-qt. baking dish. Put in oven to keep hot while preparing topping. Make ½ recipe Shortcake dough from Basic Recipe (p. 10)— except omit sugar. Roll into circle to fit top of baking dish. Make slashes near center. Place over hot filling. Bake *about 15 min. 4 to 6 servings.*

Meat Ball Pie with Pinwheel Biscuits

A switch on popular meat balls—so good with green salad.

½ lb. ground beef
½ tsp. salt
1 tbsp. catsup or chili sauce
1 egg
2 tbsp. fat
2 cups cooked mixed vegetables
3 tbsp. Bisquick
½ tsp. salt
2 cups liquid (milk plus meat stock or vegetable liquid)
½ recipe Biscuit dough
2 tbsp. catsup or chili sauce

Heat oven to 450° (hot). Mix beef, ½ tsp. salt, 1 tbsp. catsup and egg. Shape gently into 8 balls, about 1½″ in diameter. If mixture is too soft to shape, work in 1 to 2 tbsp. Bisquick. Brown in fat. Place vegetables in greased 2-qt. baking dish. Arrange meat balls on top. Blend Bisquick and ½ tsp. salt into fat remaining in skillet. Gradually stir in liquid. Bring to boil over low heat, stirring constantly. Boil 1 min. Pour over meat balls and vegetables in baking dish. Place in oven to heat while making ½ recipe Biscuit dough from Basic Recipe (p. 7). Roll dough into 8″ sq. Spread with 2 tbsp. catsup. Roll up; seal well by pinching edge of dough into roll. Cut in 12 pinwheel biscuits. Immediately arrange pinwheels on top of hot mixture; bake *15 to 20 min. 4 to 5 servings.*

TUNA FISH WITH A MAGIC TWIST

Short Tuna Pasties

Individual tuna pasties served with creamy mushroom sauce.

    1 can (7 oz.) tuna
    1 tbsp. dry parsley flakes
    1 small onion, minced
    1½ tsp. Worcestershire sauce
    ½ tsp. salt
    ⅛ tsp. pepper
    ¼ cup mayonnaise
    2 recipes Short Pie dough
    Mushroom Sauce (below)

Heat oven to 425° (hot). Mix tuna, seasonings and mayonnaise; set aside. Make 2 times Short Pie dough from Basic Recipe (p. 15). Divide into 8 equal parts. Flatten 4 parts into 5″ circles on ungreased baking sheet. Top each with an equal amount of tuna mixture. Press remaining 4 parts into 5″ circles on small squares of waxed paper. Invert paper and dough on top of filling; ease off paper. Seal edges with a fork. Cut a design on top to allow steam to escape. Bake *about 15 min.* Serve warm with Mushroom Sauce.

Mushroom Sauce

    1 can (10½ oz.) cream of
      mushroom soup
    ½ cup milk
    ½ tsp. Worcestershire sauce
    2 tbsp. finely chopped pimiento
    1 tbsp. dry parsley flakes.

Blend all ingredients; heat.

Tuna-Broccoli Casserole

    1 pkg. frozen broccoli
    1 can (7 oz.) tuna, drained and
      broken
    1 can (10½ oz.) cream of
      mushroom soup
    ½ cup milk
    ⅛ tsp. salt
    Biscuit dough

Heat oven to 450° (hot). Cook broccoli until almost tender following pkg. directions. Cut broccoli into bite-sized pieces and place in greased 9x9x2″ sq. pan. Cover broccoli with tuna. Mix soup, milk and salt together and pour over top. Make Biscuit dough from Basic Recipe (p. 7). Drop by teaspoonfuls over mixture in pan. Bake *15 min.,* or until golden brown. Serve hot. *6 servings.*

LENTEN SUPPER MENU
Spicy Tomato Juice
Short Tuna Pasties (left)
French Cut Green Beans
with Almonds
Grapefruit and Endive Salad
Velvet Crumb Cupcakes
with Pineapple Cream (p. 39)
Coffee   Milk

BISCUITS AND ROLLS
FOR ALL DINNER OCCASIONS

Make Biscuit Dough from Basic Recipe (p. 7)—except for . . .

Quick Parkerhouse Rolls:
Roll ¼″ thick. Cut with 2½″ cutter. Butter lightly and fold over. Place close together in ungreased 9x1½″ round layer or 9x9x2″ sq. pan. *Makes 12 to 16.*

Tiny Hot Biscuits: Roll dough ½″ thick. Cut with 1″ cutter. Bake close together until lightly browned.

Christmas Biscuits: Fold ¼ cup cut-up pimiento or ¼ cup chopped parsley into dough. Roll ½″ thick. Cut with small biscuit cutter. Arrange close together in shape of Christmas tree on foil-lined baking sheet. Place biscuits close enough so they will touch when baked. After baking slide foil onto serving plate; crimp foil to follow shape of tree.

Celery Biscuits: Mix 1½ tsp. celery salt in with the Bisquick. (See picture, p. 40)

Buttermilk Biscuits: Use buttermilk for liquid in dough. It may be necessary to use a few additional tbsp. buttermilk to make dough of soft consistency.

Cranberry Drop Biscuits:
Fold ½ cup canned jellied cranberry sauce, finely cubed, into dough. Drop by spoonfuls onto greased baking sheet. *Makes 12 med. or 18 small biscuits.*

Poppy Seed Cheese Rolls:
Add ½ cup grated sharp cheese to dough. Roll out ¼″ thick (or less). Cut with 1¼″ biscuit cutter. Make a crease across each round, just a little off center, with back of knife. Spread lightly with melted butter. Fold larger part over smaller so top slightly overlaps under edge. Press edges together. Brush tops with mixture of 1 egg yolk, beaten with 2 tbsp. water. Sprinkle with poppy seeds. Place on baking sheet. *Makes about 2 doz.*

ADD A FANCY TOUCH TO FAMILY FARE

Onion Biscuit Squares
(See picture, p. 40)
Fluffy biscuit squares topped with tasty onion custard.

    2 cups sliced onions
    2 tbsp. fat
    ½ tsp. salt
    dash of pepper
    Biscuit dough
    1 egg
    ½ cup commercial sour cream
    ¼ tsp. salt

Heat oven to 450° (hot). Brown onions in fat. Sprinkle with ½ tsp. salt, pepper. Make Biscuit dough from Basic Recipe (p. 7). Roll into 10″ sq. Pat firmly into greased 8x8x2″ pan. Top with cooked onions. Beat rest of ingredients together; pour over onions. Bake *about 20 min.*, or until lightly browned. Cut in squares; serve with pot roast and gravy.

Celery Crescents
Crunchy-good to serve with steak, a roast, or brown, crisp hash.

Heat oven to 450° (hot). Make Biscuit dough from Basic Recipe (p. 7). Roll into 12″ circle. Brush lightly with melted butter or margarine. Cut in 16 pie-shaped wedges. Roll up tightly, beginning at wide side. Place on baking sheet, point underneath. Shape into crescents by pulling the two ends and bringing them around in a curved shape. Brush tops with melted butter. Sprinkle with celery seeds and a little salt. Bake *10 to 12 min. Makes 16.*

Rich Dinner Biscuits
Make Biscuits from Basic Recipe (p. 7)—except use cream in place of milk in dough.

OR

Use only ½ cup milk and add 3 tbsp. vegetable oil in dough.

OR

Cut ¼ cup soft butter or margarine into Bisquick before adding milk.

Southern Chicken Bread
An old-fashioned delicacy made with drippings.

    1½ cups Bisquick
    ½ cup corn meal
    ¾ cup cream

Mix Bisquick and corn meal. Stir in cream. Knead on lightly floured surface. Roll out ⅜″ thick. Cut into rounds, squares or diamonds. Place in frying pan with small amount of fried chicken drippings. Fry over medium heat until delicately browned. Turn; brown other side. Add more fat as needed. Serve with fried chicken and gravy. *Makes about 1½ doz. pieces.*

Sour Cream Chive Biscuits
Heat oven to 450° (hot). Make Biscuits from Basic Recipe (p. 7)—except substitute ⅔ cup commercial sour cream and ⅓ cup water for the milk; add 1 tbsp. chopped fresh or frozen chives.

Beaten Raisin Bread
(See picture, p. 40)

Hearty, tender, moist—a bread specialty that makes wonderful breakfast toast, too.

> 1 pkg. active dry yeast
> 1¼ cups warm water (not hot 110 to 115°)
> 2 tbsp. sugar
> 4 cups Bisquick
> ⅔ cup raisins

In mixer bowl, dissolve yeast in warm water. Add sugar and half of Bisquick. Beat 2 min. medium speed on mixer or 300 vigorous strokes by hand. Scrape sides and bottom of bowl frequently. Add remaining Bisquick and raisins; blend well with spoon until smooth. Scrape batter from sides of bowl. Cover with a cloth and let rise in warm place (85°) until double, about 30 min. (If kitchen is cool, place dough on a rack over a bowl of hot water and cover completely with a towel.) Stir down batter by beating about 25 strokes. Spread batter evenly in greased loaf pan, 8½x4½x2½″. Batter will be sticky. Smooth out top of loaf by flouring hands and patting into shape. Again, let rise in warm place (85°) until batter reaches ½″ from top of pan, 30 to 40 min.

Heat oven to 375° (quick mod.). Bake *45 to 50 min.*, or until well browned. To test loaf, tap top crust —it should sound hollow. Immediately remove from pan. Place on cooling rack. Brush top with shortening. Cool before cutting.

Zesty, spicy flavors make these breads a "conversation piece" at dinnertime.

Follow Beaten Raisin Bread (left) —except omit raisins and for . . .

Cheese Bread: Add ⅓ cup grated sharp cheese and 2 tbsp. finely cut pimiento with second addition of Bisquick.

Caraway Bread: Add 2 tsp. caraway seeds, 1 tsp. crumbled sage and ½ tsp. nutmeg with second addition of Bisquick.

Cinnamon Bread: Slightly blend a mixture of 2 tbsp. sugar and 2 tsp. cinnamon into dough just before spreading in pan.

Hurry-up Yeast Rolls
> ¾ cup warm water (not hot— 110 to 115°)
> 1 pkg. active dry yeast
> 2½ cups Bisquick

Dissolve yeast in water. Mix in Bisquick. Beat vigorously. Turn dough onto surface well dusted with flour. Knead until smooth, about 20 times. Shape, as desired, into crescents, rolls, etc. Place on lightly greased baking sheet. Cover with cloth. Let rise about 1 hr., or until double. *Heat oven to 400°* (mod. hot). Bake *10 to 15 min.*, or until a rich golden brown. Brush with butter after baking.

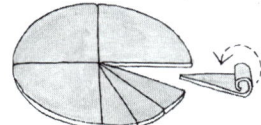

To Shape Crescents: Roll dough into 12″ circle. Cut in 16 wedges. Beginning at wide side, roll toward point. Place on greased baking sheet with point underneath. *Makes 16.*

BRING ON THE DESSERT

Chocolate Short Pie

Baked Short Pie shell
½ cup Bisquick
¾ cup sugar
⅓ cup cocoa
1 cup cold water
2 cups milk
1 tsp. vanilla

Prepare baked Short Pie Shell from Basic Recipe (p. 15). Cool. Mix Bisquick, sugar and cocoa. Gradually stir in cold water. Add milk; cook over medium heat, stirring constantly, until mixture comes to a boil. Boil 1 min. Add vanilla. Cool. Pour into Short Pie shell. Top with whipped cream.

Short Pie Tarts

Easy but with a fancy look!

Short Pie dough
1 cup commercial sour cream
or whipped cream
¼ cup brown sugar
1 pt. fresh strawberries

Make Short Pie dough from Basic Recipe (p. 15). Divide into 6 parts. Pat out each piece on a 5″ circle of heavy-duty aluminum foil (use top of coffee can to measure foil pieces). Make tart shells by folding up an inch of foil and pinching in four corners. Place tart pans on baking sheet. Bake *7 to 9 min.*, or until lightly browned. Cool. Remove foil carefully. Serve tart shells filled with a mixture of cream, brown sugar and strawberries.

Strawberry Glacé Short Pie

An elegant company dessert.

Baked Short Pie Shell
1 qt. strawberries
1 cup water
1 cup sugar
3 tbsp. cornstarch

Prepare baked Short Pie Shell from Basic Recipe (p. 15). Cool. Wash, drain and hull strawberries. Simmer 1 cup of the berries and ⅔ cup water for 3 min., or until berries start to break up. Blend sugar, cornstarch, remaining ⅛ cup water; add to boiling mixture. Boil 1 min., stirring constantly. Cool. Place remaining 3 cups of berries in Short Pie shell. Cover with cooked mixture. Refrigerate until firm, about 2 hr. Serve with whipped cream or ice cream.

OCTOBER NIGHT BUFFET

Baked Ham

Glazed Sweet Potatoes

Sliced Cucumbers
in Sour Cream

Crisp Relish Tray

Rich Dinner Biscuits (p. 48)
with Orange Marmalade

Chocolate Short Pie (left)

Coffee   Milk

Peach Pecan Shortcake

Creamy, crunchy, juicy—a smooth harmony of perfect flavors.

Make the individual Shortcakes from Basic Recipe (p. 10)—except add ½ cup chopped pecans to dough. Divide each baked shortcake in half. Arrange sweetened sliced peaches (fresh or frozen) and chilled sweetened whipped cream between the layers and on top. Garnish with pecan halves. (One pkg. frozen peaches and 1 cup whipping cream, whipped, will serve 6.)

Apple or Peach Crisp

A homey, all-time favorite.

4 cups peeled sliced apples or peaches
2 tbsp. water
¼ to ⅓ cup sugar (depending on tartness of fruit)
1¼ cups Bisquick
½ cup sugar
½ tsp. cinnamon
1 egg
¼ cup butter or margarine, melted

Heat oven to 400° (mod. hot). Place fruit in greased 10x6x1½" oblong or 8x8x2" sq. pan. Sprinkle water and sugar over fruit. Mix Bisquick, sugar and cinnamon. Beat egg thoroughly. Pour slowly over Bisquick mixture in a thin stream, stirring constantly with a fork until crumbly. Sprinkle mixture over fruit. Pour butter over all. Bake *about 25 min.*, or until brown. Serve hot or cold with milk or cream. *6 to 8 servings.*

Pear à la Crème

Custard and pears in a rich, cooky-like crust.

2 cups Bisquick
½ cup sugar
¼ cup butter or margarine
6 to 9 canned pear halves (depending on size)
2 egg yolks, slightly beaten
1 cup sweet OR commercial sour cream
nutmeg
¼ cup slivered almonds, if desired

Heat oven to 375° (quick mod.). Mix Bisquick with 2 tbsp. of sugar. Cut in butter until mixture looks like meal. Pat evenly over bottom and halfway up sides of an 8x8x2" baking dish, pressing firmly. Drain pear halves; arrange over pastry in rows, cut side down, sprinkling with remaining sugar. Bake *15 min.;* pour mixture of egg yolks and cream over top. Sprinkle with nutmeg and almonds. Bake *30 min. more*, until custard is set. Serve warm. *9 servings.*

Note: Milk may be used instead of cream making a less rich dessert.

Pear Upside-Down Fudge Cake

Pears and chocolate—a gourmet combination.

- ¼ cup butter or margarine
- ½ cup brown sugar (packed)
- ½ tsp. cinnamon
- 6 canned pear halves, drained and each cut in 4 lengthwise slices
- 6 maraschino cherries, halved, if desired
- Velvet Crumb Cake batter
- ⅓ cup cocoa

Heat oven to 350° (mod.). Melt butter over low heat in bottom of 9x9x2″ sq. pan. Sprinkle with brown sugar and cinnamon. Arrange pear slices and cherries over sugar mixture; set aside. Make Velvet Crumb Cake batter from Basic Recipe (p. 11) —except add ⅓ cup cocoa to Bisquick before mixing. Pour batter over pear slices in pan. Bake *45 to 55 min.*, or until toothpick stuck in center comes out clean. Invert at once onto serving plate; allow pan to remain over top a few minutes so sugar mixture will run down over cake. Serve warm, plain, with whipped or commercial sour cream.

FAMILY CELEBRATION
DINNER
Broiled Lamb Chops
Buttered new Potatoes
Lime Gelatin Mold
Beaten Bread (p. 49)
Pear Upside-Down
Fudge Cake (above)
Coffee   Milk

Mocha Spice Velvet Crumb Cake

A tempting blend of coffee and spice flavors.

Heat oven to 350° (mod.). Make Velvet Crumb Cake batter from Basic Recipe (p. 11)—except add ½ tsp. cinnamon, ¼ tsp. each nutmeg, cloves, allspice, 1 tbsp. powdered instant coffee. Pour into prepared pan. Bake *35 to 40 min.* Top with Mocha Cream (below).

Mocha Cream

- 1 cup whipping cream
- ¼ cup sifted confectioners' sugar
- 1 tsp. powdered instant coffee

Whip cream. Fold in confectioners sugar and coffee. (If desired, all ingredients may be mixed in bowl, chilled until serving time, then beaten stiff.)

Sour Cream Velvet Crumb Cake

. . . with strawberries and brown sugar.

Heat oven to 350° (mod.). Make Velvet Crumb Cake batter from Basic Recipe (p. 11)—except substitute ¼ cup commercial sour cream for ¼ cup of the milk in the first mixing period. Bake *35 to 40 min.* Serve warm with Strawberry Sour Cream Topping (below).

Strawberry Sour Cream Topping:

Mix 1 cup commercial sour cream, ¼ cup brown sugar (packed) and 1 pt. fresh strawberries.

Berry Puffs

Use raspberries, blueberries or blackberries.

¾ cup berries
6 tbsp. sugar
1 cup Bisquick
½ cup sugar
1 egg, beaten
⅓ cup milk

Grease well 6 little custard cups or pudding molds. Place 2 tbsp. berries and 1 tbsp. sugar in each cup. Mix Bisquick and ½ cup sugar. Stir in mixture of egg and milk. Pour batter over berries, filling each a scant ⅔ full. Tie waxed paper over top of each cup. Steam ½ hr. (See p. 64). Serve with cream. *6 servings.*

Pecan Fingers

For a quick dessert—serve with ice cream.

1 cup Bisquick
¼ cup soft butter or margarine
¼ cup chopped pecans
1 tbsp. sugar
½ tsp. almond extract or vanilla
3 tbsp. boiling water

Heat oven to 375° (quick mod.). In mixing bowl, blend Bisquick, butter, nuts, sugar and flavoring. Add boiling water; stir vigorously with fork until dough forms a ball and cleans the bowl. Shape dough in 24 fingers 2½″ long. Place on ungreased baking sheet. Bake *10 to 12 min.* While warm, roll each finger in granulated or confectioners' sugar. *Makes 2 doz. cookies.*

Baked Cranberry Pudding

Rich and colorful—from old New England.

2 cups Bisquick
1 cup sugar
3 tbsp. melted shortening or vegetable oil
⅔ cup milk
1 egg
2 cups whole cranberries (fresh or frozen)

Heat oven to 350° (mod.). Mix Bisquick and sugar. Stir in shortening, milk and egg until well blended. Fold in cranberries. Pour into greased 9x9x2″ sq. pan. Bake *about 40 min.*, or until nicely browned and loosened from sides of pan. Serve with warm Butter Sauce (below). *9 servings.*

Butter Sauce: Mix ½ cup butter, 1 cup sugar and ¾ cup light cream in saucepan. Cook 5 min. over low heat. Be careful not to scorch.

Baked Blueberry Pudding:

Make Baked Cranberry Pudding (above)—except use 2 cups fresh blueberries or 1 pkg. (12 oz.) frozen blueberries, thawed, in place of cranberries. Serve warm with Lemon Butter Sauce (remove Butter Sauce from heat; blend in grated rind of one lemon) or sweetened whipped cream with grated lemon rind folded in.

BEGINNERS'
LUCK

"... I was introduced to Bisquick 6 years ago as a bride—a very dear friend gave me an assortment of baking dishes and a large box of Bisquick and I've used it ever since

Mrs. Paul J. King
San Jose, California

"... I am a retired bachelor and I do my own cooking, much of it with Bisquick"

Joseph D. Deschler
Dayton, Ohio

Brides, bachelors, teenagers—beginning cooks of all ages—write to tell us that Bisquick brings them luck! Learning to cook can be fun when everything you bake turns out perfectly the very first time. From the Basic Recipes in Chapter One straight through to the final page, the Bisquick bakings in this little book are sure to succeed. And here in the following pages are extra-quick and "lucky" dishes—easy to make, fancy to look at and all good to the very last bite.

Fresh Tomato Shortcake, p. 56.

DELICIOUS "QUICKIE" DISHES

Fresh Tomato Shortcake

(See picture, p. 54)

Bacon, tomato and cheese flavors— good with lettuce wedges.

Make 6 individual Shortcakes from Basic Recipe (p. 10)—except omit sugar. While shortcakes are baking, prepare Cheese Sauce (right). Broil 6 slices bacon. Slice about 5 peeled, ripe, medium-sized tomatoes. Split and butter warm shortcakes. Place tomato slices between layers and on top. Sprinkle with salt and pepper to taste. Serve with hot Cheese Sauce (right) and garnish each serving with a crisp bacon strip. *6 servings.*

Asparagus Shortcake with Cheese Sauce

Serve with cold sliced ham for a satisfying meal.

Heat oven to 450° (hot). Make Biscuit dough from Basic Recipe (p. 7). Roll ¼″ thick. Cut into 4 or 5″ rounds. Bake *about 10 min.* Split. Serve sandwich-fashion with about 5 freshly cooked asparagus spears between biscuit halves. Pour Cheese Sauce (right) over top. *4 to 5 servings.*

Cheese Sauce

¼ cup butter or margarine
¼ cup Bisquick
½ tsp. salt
¼ tsp. pepper
¼ tsp. mustard, if desired
2 cups milk
2 cups grated sharp cheese

Melt butter over low heat. Blend in Bisquick and seasonings. Cook over low heat, stirring until smooth and bubbly. Take off heat. Stir in milk. Bring to boil; boil 1 min., stirring constantly. Stir in cheese until melted.

Pancheesies

Cheese-filled pancake sandwiches. Teen-agers love them.

Make Pancakes from Basic Recipe (p. 8). When pancakes are turned, place thin slice of cheese on top of half of the pancakes. When baked, place a plain pancake on top of cheese. It will melt the cheese. Serve immediately with creamed meat, fish or vegetables.

Variation: Place crisply fried bacon on cheese and cover with second pancake.

FRIDAY NIGHT SUPPER

Pancheesies (above) with
Creamed Tuna Fish
Buttered Broccoli
Crisp Relishes
Fresh Fruit
Pudding Cookies (p. 59)
Coffee   Milk

Emergency Chicken Stew and Dumplings

Ideal answer to unexpected guests.

1 pkg. (12 oz.) frozen mixed vegetables
1 can (10½ oz.) cream of celery soup
1 can (10½ oz.) cream of chicken soup
1 soup can of water
⅛ tsp. celery seeds
1 can (10½ oz.) chicken cut in bite-size pieces
¼ cup Bisquick
¼ cup water
salt and pepper to taste
½ recipe Dumpling dough

Cook frozen mixed vegetables in ½ cup boiling salted water 7 min. Combine soups, water and celery seeds. Add vegetables with liquid and bring to a boil. Mix in chicken. Blend Bisquick and water; stir in and cook until thickened. Add salt and pepper. Make half Basic Dumpling Recipe (p. 14). Drop by spoonfuls onto hot chicken mixture. Cook over low heat *10 min.*, uncovered, and *10 min.*, covered. To serve: lift off dumplings, ladle chicken stew into individual serving dishes and put one or more dumplings on top. *4 to 6 servings.*

Simple Simon Beef with Muffin Squares

Serve with a crisp green salad—and there's your dinner.

2 tbsp. chopped onion
2 tbsp. fat
1 lb. ground beef
1½ tsp. salt
dash of pepper
2 tbsp. chopped green pepper
2 cups mixed cooked vegetables
liquid from vegetables plus water to make 1½ cups
2 bouillon cubes
2 tbsp. Bisquick
¼ cup water
Muffin batter

Sauté onion in fat over medium heat; add meat and brown. Add seasonings, vegetables, liquid and bouillon cubes; simmer 15 min. Mix Bisquick and water; slowly blend into hot mixture, stirring constantly. Cook until thick. Serve over hot split Muffin Squares (below). *6 to 8 servings.*

Muffin Squares: Heat oven to 400° (mod. hot). Make Muffin batter from Basic Recipe (p. 13)—except omit sugar and add ⅛ tsp. poultry seasoning. Spread batter in greased 8x8x2" sq. pan. Bake *about 20 min.* To serve, cut into squares.

> ### "INSTANT" COMPANY SUPPER
> Emergency Chicken Stew with Dumplings (left)
> Lettuce Wedges with French Dressing
> Peach Jam Cake (p. 59)
> Coffee or Milk

BREADS A BRIDE CAN BAKE

Biscuit Bread

Heat oven to 450° (hot). Make Biscuit dough from Basic Recipe (p. 7) —except do not knead. Spread on greased baking sheet to make an oblong, about 10x8″. Spread top with 1 tbsp. soft butter or margarine. Bake *10 min.* Serve hot, broken in pieces or cut in squares.

Variations:

• Add ¼ cup raisins, 2 tbsp. sugar to dough. Sprinkle top with mixture of cinnamon and sugar.

• Sprinkle top with garlic powder or salt.

• Add 1 tbsp. instant dried onion to dough. Sprinkle top with poppy seeds.

• Add 1 tsp. caraway seeds to dough. Sprinkle top with salt and paprika.

• Spread dough in a circle; bake, cut in wedges and serve.

• After baking, spread top with ½ cup strawberry jam (or other jam or jelly).

> Making perfect biscuits and muffins is easy and fun when you follow the Basic Recipes for Biscuits (p. 7) and Muffins (p. 13). Serve hot from the oven with butter for any meal of the day.

Glazed Jam Puffs

Surprise! There's jam inside.

    2 cups Bisquick
    2 tbsp. sugar
    ¼ cup soft butter or margarine
    ⅔ cup milk
    10 tsp. raspberry jam

Heat oven to 450° (hot). Mix Bisquick, sugar and butter. Add milk all at once; stir into a soft dough. Beat 20 strokes. Place a tablespoonful of dough in 10 paper-lined medium-sized muffin cups. Top with a teaspoonful of raspberry jam. Drop a tablespoonful of dough over jam. Bake *10 to 15 min.*, or until golden brown. Remove from pan immediately. Frost with Easy Creamy Icing (below). Serve warm.

Easy Creamy Icing

Blend 1 cup sifted confectioners' sugar, a pinch of salt, ½ tsp. vanilla and liquid to make easy to spread (about 1 tbsp. water or 1½ tbsp. cream).

Cinnamon Biscuit Balls

Heat oven to 450° (hot). Make Biscuit dough from Basic Recipe (p. 7). Drop a teaspoonful at a time into a mixture of 2 tbsp. sugar and 1 tsp. cinnamon. Place on lightly greased baking sheet. Bake *8 to 10 min.* Makes 2 doz. small cinnamon balls.

EASY "SUCCESS" DESSERTS

Sheet Shortcake
Shortcake Short Cut!

Heat oven to 450° (hot). Make Shortcake dough from Basic Recipe (p. 10). Pat or roll on greased baking sheet into a rectangle, 12x8″. Spread with 2 tbsp. butter or margarine; sprinkle with 2 tbsp. sugar and ¼ tsp. nutmeg. Bake *10 to 12 min.*, or until lightly browned. Cut in 6 serving pieces. Top with sweetened berries or peaches. Serve warm.

Pudding Cookies
Rolled buttery sugar cookies . . . thin, crisp and tender. Made with Bisquick and instant pudding mix.

    ¾ cup Bisquick
    1 pkg. instant pudding mix
    ¼ cup vegetable oil
    1 egg

Heat oven to 350° (mod.). Mix ingredients together until dough forms a ball. Shape into balls, using 1 tsp. dough for each. Place on ungreased baking sheet. Flatten to about 2″ with hand. Bake *8 min. Makes 2½ to 3 doz. cookies.*

Streusel Velvet Crumb Cake
Favorite topping for a cake which is really too delicate to support a conventional thick icing.

Heat oven to 350° (mod.). Grease and flour an 8x8x2″ sq. pan. Make Velvet Crumb Cake batter from Basic Recipe (p. 11). Pour batter into prepared pan and sprinkle with Streusel Topping: Mix together ¼ cup Bisquick, 2 tsp. cinnamon, 2 tbsp. brown sugar and 1 tbsp. cold butter or margarine. Bake *35 to 40 min.*

Peach or Apricot Jam Cake
Fancy topping made easy.

Make Velvet Crumb Cake from Basic Recipe (p. 11). After baking, spread ½ cup apricot or peach jam over hot cake. Serve warm.

Ice Cream Sundae Pies
Party-pretty.

Heat oven to 450° (hot). Make Short Pie dough from Basic Recipe (p. 15) —except add ½ tsp. almond or vanilla flavoring. Divide and roll into 12 balls; pat each into a 3″ round on a baking sheet. Bake *6 to 8 min.* Cool. Top each round with ice cream and your favorite sundae sauce or sweetened fruit.

REAL OLD-FASHIONED
FAVORITES

"... I always wondered how to make rolled dumplings* like my grandmother did and, of course, it's hard to get recipes from grandmothers — they didn't ever measure anything. Someone told me to make them like biscuits, adding an egg. I tried this with Bisquick and it worked perfectly. They are delicious and just like Grandma's."

Mrs. David A. Porter
St. Louis, Missouri

Every now and then, we find in our mailbox a love letter about foods from the past—fresh doughnuts made in a sunny farmhouse kitchen, chicken and dumplings bubbling on a big wood range or golden-crusted strawberry shortcake with real country cream. This is the kind of eating, remembered from childhood, that we still enjoy even in today's wonderful world of convenience foods. And here are easy, new-fashioned Bisquick recipes — from flapjacks to apple slump to steamed cranberry pudding—for baking the good homemade favorites of long ago.

*See page 63 for Betty Crocker's Rolled Egg Dumplings.

Chicken Fricassee with Bisquick Dumplings, p. 63;
Old-Fashioned Strawberry Shortcake, p. 65.

Pancakes, a dish almost as old as time itself, first came to America with the Dutch settlers. Now, thick and hearty or delicately thin and light, they are eaten at morning, noon or night!

Buttermilk Pancakes

These flavorful, tender-textured cakes are descended from pioneer days.

    2 cups Bisquick
    1 tsp. soda
    1 egg
    2 cups buttermilk

Mix all ingredients with rotary beater until smooth. Batter will be fairly thick. Spoon onto medium hot griddle. Grease griddle, if necessary. It may be necessary to spread batter with spoon if it is too thick. Turn cakes when bubbles appear and edges begin to dry. Serve with syrup. *Makes about twenty 4″ pancakes.*

Cornmeal Buttermilk Pancakes

An authentic Early American favorite served with maple syrup.

Follow recipe for Buttermilk Pancakes (above)—except use only 1½ cups Bisquick and add ½ cup cornmeal.

Bisquick Raised Flapjacks

A real lumberjack's meal—Ideal Sunday night supper with hot tomato juice appetizer, plenty of coffee or tea.

    1 pkg. active dry yeast
    ¼ cup warm water (not hot—
      110 to 115°)
    1 egg
    1⅔ cups milk
    2 cups Bisquick

Dissolve yeast in warm water. Beat egg, milk and Bisquick with rotary beater until smooth. Stir in dissolved yeast. Cover; let stand at room temperature for 1½ hr. *Do not stir.* Bake on hot griddle. Grease if necessary. Turn cakes when bubbles appear and edges begin to dry. *Makes about twenty 4″ cakes.*

Sour Cream Pancakes

A country-good, old-time favorite.

    2 cups Bisquick
    1 egg
    1 cup water
    ⅔ cup commercial sour cream

Beat all ingredients together with rotary beater. Spoon batter onto hot griddle. Grease griddle, if necessary. Turn pancakes when bubbles appear and edges begin to dry. Beat batter between bakings. *Makes about twenty 4″ pancakes.*

Chicken Fricassee with Bisquick Dumplings

(See picture, p. 60)

Sunday dinner "down on the farm."

1 stewing chicken (4 to 5 lb.)
   cut up
¼ cup fat
2 sprigs parsley
4 celery tops
1 carrot, sliced
1 slice of onion
2 tsp. salt
⅛ tsp. pepper
Dumpling dough

Brown chicken slowly in fat. Place in kettle with just enough boiling water to cover. Add rest of ingredients except dumplings. Boil 5 min.; turn down heat and simmer until tender (2 to 3 hr.). Make Dumplings from Basic Recipe (p. 14) and drop on simmering stew. Remove dumplings and chicken to a platter; keep hot while making Gravy (below). Pour Gravy over chicken and dumplings and serve. *8 servings.*

Gravy: Leave chicken broth (about) 4 cups) in kettle over low heat. Skim off excess fat. Mix ½ cup Bisquick and 1 cup milk or cold water to a smooth paste. Stir into broth. Cook until thickened (about 15 min.), stirring occasionally. Season to taste.

DUMPLING VARIATIONS

Curry Dumplings: Add ½ tsp. curry powder to dumpling dough.

Herb Dumplings: Add 1 tsp. *each* poultry seasoning, instant dried onion, celery flakes and parsley flakes to dumpling dough.

Potato Pancakes

Bisquick version of an Old World dish —lacy, crispy, golden brown. Traditionally served with pot roast.

2 cups finely grated raw
   potatoes, well drained
¼ cup milk
2 eggs, well beaten
¼ cup Bisquick
1¼ tsp. salt

Mix all ingredients together. Drop by tablespoonfuls into ¼″ hot fat in skillet. Sauté about 3 min. on each side, turning only when golden brown. *Makes 18 pancakes.*

Rolled Egg Dumplings

A delightful old-fashioned light dumpling like those our grandmothers used to make.

1 cup Bisquick
1 egg
1 tbsp. milk

Mix ingredients thoroughly with fork. Turn dough onto well floured cloth-covered board. Knead for 2 to 3 min., until smooth and elastic. Roll into 12x6″ rectangle and cut into 12 strips, 6x1″. Drop into boiling stew, pushing gently with fork to coat on both sides with broth. (Strips may overlap during cooking.) Cook over low heat *10 min.* uncovered and *10 min.* covered. *Makes 12 dumplings.*

Apple Pan Dowdy

Heat oven to 400° (mod. hot). Place 6 apples, pared and cored in 8x8x2″ sq. or 10x6x1½″ oblong pan. Sprinkle with 1 to 2 tbsp. water, ½ cup sugar and 1 tsp. cinnamon. Make Shortcake dough from Basic Recipe (p. 10). Roll or pat to fit top of pan and place over apples. Prick dough with fork to allow steam to escape. Bake about *40 min. 6 servings.*

Apple Slump

Louisa May Alcott's house was named for the original of this famous old dessert, "Apple Slump,"—really an upside-down dowdy.

Make Apple Pan Dowdy (above)— except pare and slice the apples into a greased 2-qt. baking dish. When baked, invert on a serving plate and serve hot with cream.

Blueberry or other Berry

Slump: Place 1 qt. fresh berries, 1½ cups sugar and 1 cup water in saucepan. Bring to boil. Pour into greased baking dish. Proceed as for Apple Slump.

Steamed Cranberry Pudding

An old New England dish— dates back to Colonial times.

> ½ cup sorghum or molasses
> ½ cup warm water
> 2 tsp. soda
> 1¼ cups raw cranberries
> 1½ cups Bisquick

Mix sorghum, water and soda. Add cranberries and Bisquick; mix well. Pour into greased and floured 1-qt. mold or 2-lb. coffee can (⅔ full). Tie waxed paper loosely over top. Steam 2½ to 3 hr. Unmold onto serving platter. Serve hot with hot Easy Vanilla or Rum Sauce (below). *8 servings.*

Easy Vanilla or Rum Sauce: Mix 1 cup sugar and ½ cup cream. Heat but do not boil. When ready to serve, beat in ½ cup melted butter or margarine with rotary beater. Add 1 tsp. vanilla or rum flavoring.

To Steam Successfully: Place mold on rack in tightly covered steamer over water already boiling. Steam must surround mold. Have enough water to last through steaming . . . but not enough to touch mold. Do not lift lid before pudding is cooked or it will fall.

To Improvise a Steamer: Arrange a rack 2″ above bottom of roaster or deep kettle with tight fitting cover.

DESSERTS FROM THE GOOD OLD DAYS

The All-Time Favorite
(See picture, p. 60)

That good, old-time, all-American dessert—Strawberry Shortcake—is still first choice in most families.

Make shortcakes from Basic Shortcake Recipe (p. 10). Serve with sweetened fruit and cream.

Doughnuts or Fried Balls
From an old farmhouse kitchen recipe.

> 2 cups Bisquick
> ¼ cup sugar
> ⅓ cup milk
> 1 tsp. vanilla
> 1 egg
> ¼ tsp. *each* cinnamon and nutmeg, if desired

Heat fat to 375°. Mix ingredients until well blended. Turn onto lightly floured surface; knead about 10 times. Roll out ⅜" thick. Cut with floured doughnut cutter. Fry in hot fat until golden brown, about 1 min. to a side. Take from fat and drain on absorbent paper. *Makes about 12 doughnuts.*

Fried Balls: Drop scant teaspoonfuls of dough into hot fat. *Makes 32 balls, 1¼" in diameter.*

Fruit Cobbler
From "cobble up"—meaning to mix in a hurry.

> 1 can (1 lb. 13 oz.) fruit and juice OR 3 cups fresh fruit sweetened and ¾ cup water
> 1 tbsp. cornstarch dissolved in 2 tbsp. cold water
> ½ recipe Shortcake dough

Heat oven to 400° (mod. hot). Heat fruit and liquid; blend in cornstarch mixture. Boil 1 min. Pour into 2-qt. baking dish. Dot with butter. Make Shortcake dough from Basic Recipe (p. 10). Drop by spoonfuls over fruit. Bake *about 20 min.* Serve hot with light cream. *6 to 8 servings.*

Rhubarb Fluffs

> 2½ lb. fresh pink rhubarb, cut in 1" pieces (about 7½ cups)
> ⅔ cup water
> 1 to 1½ cups sugar
> Dumpling dough

Bring to boil rhubarb, water and sugar in deep 4-qt. saucepan. Make Dumpling dough from Basic Recipe (p. 14). Drop spoonfuls of dumpling dough onto rhubarb. Cook uncovered, over medium heat *10 min.* and *10 min.* covered. Serve warm with cream. *6 to 8 servings.*

COMPANY'S
COMING

"... Bisquick is a life-and-company saver. When I get unexpected company, I mix up a coffee cake, tarts or velvet crumb cake..."

Mrs. Al Smith
St. Paul, Minnesota

"... to ask you to help me make a coffee cake for about 25 people out of your Bisquick. I have a breakfast meeting coming up and would like to surprise the members."

Mrs. W. Lauer
Hoboken, New Jersey

Party brunches, neighborhood coffee parties, big or little teas and glamorous dessert parties—these are just a few of the popular carefree ways a busy homemaker entertains today. No wonder our mail is filled with requests for party and snack foods that are easy, "different" and as delicious as they are good to look at. From appetizers to pie, sandwiches to pizza—here are praise-winning Bisquick recipes to make party-giving easy for you and wonderful fun for your guests!

See page 93 for Coffee Cake for a Party

Butterscotch Meringue Cake, p. 78; Orange Short Pie, p. 80;
Cherry-raisin Coffee Cake, p. 75.

COME FOR BRUNCH!

Pancakes that puff—delicate, airy-light and tender as cake.

Puff Pancakes

2 eggs
1 cup milk
2⅓ cups Bisquick
2 tbsp. sugar
¼ cup vegetable oil or melted shortening

Beat eggs with rotary beater until soft peaks form. This takes a few minutes, but it is important. Blend in milk; add Bisquick and sugar. Mix just until thoroughly dampened. Fold in oil. Spoon onto medium-hot ungreased griddle. When puffed up, and bubbles begin to break, bake on other side. Serve with syrup. *Makes 15 to 20 pancakes.*

For richer pancakes, use 20% cream in place of milk.

GOURMET BREAKFAST TREAT

Garnish each piping hot stack of puff pancakes with a generous spoonful of commercial sour cream. Serve with syrup. Very special!

PUFF PANCAKE VARIATIONS

Follow recipe (left)—except:

Pecan Puff Pancakes: fold ¾ to 1 cup finely chopped pecans or walnuts into batter. Serve with Maple Rum-Flavored Syrup (p.22).

Bacon Puff Pancakes: add 4 strips bacon, fried and crumbled, to batter. Serve with maple syrup.

Spicy Puff Pancakes: add 1 tsp. cinnamon and ½ tsp. each allspice, cloves and nutmeg to batter.

Blueberry Puff Pancakes: add 1 cup firm fresh blueberries or drained canned blueberries to batter.

Ham Puff Pancakes: add 1 to 1½ cups ground or chopped cooked ham to batter.

Corn Puff Pancakes: add 1 cup cream-style corn or drained whole kernel corn to batter. Good with grilled ham.

WEEKEND GUESTS' BRUNCH

Half Grapefruit
Corn Puff Pancakes (above)
and Maple Syrup
Grilled Ham
Scrambled Eggs with Chives
Coffee   Milk

WAFFLES AND CHICKEN

make a mid-day party meal.

Party Waffles Royal

Waffles
Creamed Chicken
⅛ tsp. poultry seasoning
1½ cups warm whole-berry
cranberry sauce

Prepare Creamed Chicken (right) —except add ⅛ tsp. poultry seasoning. Keep warm over hot water while making Waffles from Basic Recipe (p. 9). Serve by arranging 2 waffle sections sandwich-style with Creamed Chicken in center. Serve hot with warm cranberry sauce over top. *4 to 6 servings.*

Curry Waffles Royal

Prepare Creamed Chicken (right)— except add ¼ to ½ tsp. curry powder. Keep warm over hot water while making Waffles from Basic Recipe (p. 9)—except add ½ tsp. curry powder to batter. Serve hot Creamed Chicken over waffles. *4 to 6 servings.*

SUNDAY BRUNCH
Hot Spiced Apple Juice
Party Waffles Royal (above)
Ripe Olives
Coffee   Milk

Corn Waffles Royal

Prepare Creamed Chicken (below)— except add 1 can (4 oz.) sliced mushrooms and 2 tbsp. chopped pimiento. Keep warm over hot water while making Waffles from Basic Recipe (p. 9)—except add 1 cup well drained whole kernel corn to batter. Serve hot Creamed Chicken over waffles. *4 to 6 servings.*

Creamed Chicken

¼ cup butter or margarine
¼ cup Bisquick
½ tsp. salt
¼ tsp. pepper
2 cups milk
1½ to 2 cups cut-up cooked
chicken

Melt butter over low heat in heavy saucepan. Wooden spoon for stirring is a help. Blend in flour and seasonings. Cook over low heat, stirring until mixture is smooth and bubbly. Remove from heat. Stir in milk. Bring to boil, stirring constantly. Boil 1 min. Stir in chicken.

Cooked turkey may be used in place of chicken.

QUICK AND GLAMOROUS BRUNCH BREADS

Raspberry Peek-A-Boos

*Like little frosted muffins . . . these
need no butter.*

1 cup fresh raspberries
4 tbsp. sugar
½ tsp. nutmeg
½ tsp. cinnamon
2 tsp. lemon juice
2 cups Bisquick
¼ cup soft butter or margarine
⅔ cup milk

Heat oven to 450° (hot). Toss raspberries, 2 tbsp. sugar, nutmeg, cinnamon and lemon juice. Set aside.
Combine Bisquick, 2 tbsp. sugar and
butter. Add milk all at once; stir
with fork into soft dough. Beat 20
strokes. Place a tablespoonful of
dough in bottom of each of ten
paper-lined medium muffin cups. Top
with 1 tbsp. raspberry mixture. Drop
a scant tablespoonful of dough onto
berries. Bake *10 to 15 min.*, or until
golden brown. Remove Peek-A-Boos
from muffin tins immediately. When
slightly cool, frost with Easy Creamy
Icing (p. 58). *Makes 10 medium-size
Peek-A-Boos.*

Blueberry Peek-A-Boos: Substitute blueberries for raspberries.

Orange Glacé Coffee Cake

butter
sugar
2 cups Bisquick
1 tbsp. sugar
2 tbsp. butter or margarine
⅔ cup milk
1 tsp. grated orange rind

Make Glacé Topping (below). *Heat
oven to 400°* (mod. hot). Butter an
8x8x2″ pan generously; sprinkle with
sugar. Mix Bisquick, 1 tbsp. sugar,
2 tbsp. butter, milk and orange rind
in bowl; stir until moistened. Beat
vigorously 30 seconds. Pat into prepared pan. With sharp knife dipped
in flour, cut through dough to make
16 squares. Pour hot Glacé Topping
evenly over dough. Bake *20 to 25
min.*, or until well browned. Cut
squares and serve warm.

Glacé Topping: Melt ¼ cup butter or
margarine in small pan. Add 1 tsp.
grated orange rind, 2 tbsp. orange
juice and 3 tbsp. sugar. Boil rapidly
3 min., stirring occasionally.

"SPECIAL OCCASION" BREADS TO MAKE WITH YEAST

Festive Coffee Ring

½ cup warm water (not hot—
  110 to 115°)
1 pkg. active dry yeast
1 egg
1 tbsp. granulated sugar
2½ cups Bisquick
2 tbsp. butter or margarine
¼ cup brown sugar

Dissolve yeast in warm water. Add egg, sugar and Bisquick. Beat vigorously 2 min. Turn dough onto well floured surface. Knead until smooth, about 20 times. Roll into rectangle, 16x9″. Spread with butter and brown sugar. Roll up tightly beginning at wide side. Seal well by pinching edge of dough into roll. Place roll, sealed side down, on greased baking sheet. Pinch ends together making a ring. With scissors, make cuts ⅔ of way through ring at 1″ intervals. Turn each section on its side. Let rise in warm place (85°) about 1 hr. (If kitchen is cool, place dough on a rack over a bowl of hot water and cover completely with a towel.)

Heat oven to 375° (quick mod.). Bake *15 to 20 min.* Frost with Easy Creamy Icing (p. 58) while warm. Decorate with candied cherry halves and walnut halves.

Hawaiian Yeast Rolls

Make Festive Coffee Ring (left)— except after spreading the dough with butter and sugar and shaping the roll—cut roll into 12 slices. Place slices in prepared muffin cups (below). Cover with cloth and let rise in warm place (85°) 45 min. to 1 hr. *Heat oven to 400°* (mod. hot). Bake *15 min.* Invert pan and serve warm.

To Prepare Muffin Cups: Mix ¾ cup drained crushed pineapple, ½ cup brown sugar (packed) and ¼ cup soft butter. Divide among 12 large greased muffin cups.

Christmas Company Brunch will be bright with holiday cheer when you serve Festive Coffee Ring (left) or Cranberry Pancakes (p. 19).

FOR HAPPY BRUNCH-TIME ENTERTAINING

gay, informal and easy on the hostess.

Hawaiian Buffet Brunch
(See picture, pp. 72-73)

A beautiful and sumptuous party in the spirit of the Islands. Serve in a setting of flowers and greenery—indoors or out—for a colorful, exotic scene.

Watermelon Boat with Fresh Fruits
Bisquick Thin Pancakes
with Pineapple Sauce (p. 81)
Pork Sausage (p. 21)
Sautéed Chicken Livers
Tiny Coconut and
Banana Aloha Muffins (below)
Coffee

Tiny Fruit Aloha Muffins

2 cups Bisquick
¼ cup sugar
3 tbsp. soft butter or margarine
1 egg
¾ cup milk
½ cup toasted grated fresh coconut OR ½ cup well-drained crushed pineapple

Heat oven to 400° (mod. hot). Mix Bisquick and sugar; cut in butter. Add egg and milk; beat vigorously 30 seconds. Fold in coconut or pineapple. Fill tiny greased muffin pans ⅔ full. Bake *12 to 15 min.* While still warm, frost with Easy Creamy Icing (p. 58). Sprinkle either toasted fresh coconut or coarsely chopped macadamia nuts over top. *Makes 3 to 4 doz.*

Banana Muffin Variation:

Omit milk, coconut and pineapple; add 1 cup mashed *very ripe* banana to batter.

Children's Saturday Brunch Party

Invite the neighborhood youngsters and let everyone bake his own "branded" pancakes.

Fruit Punch
"Round-up" Pancakes (below)
Baked Ham or Canadian Bacon
Milk or Hot Chocolate

"Round-Up" Pancakes

Cowboy game—let every child pour his private brand in batter.

Make Pancake batter from Basic Recipe (p. 8). Let batter trickle from a teaspoon onto hot griddle to form an initial. (Initials must be made backwards to make them appear right when pancakes are served.) When bottom side of initial has browned, pour about ¼ cup of batter over initial. Bake until bubbles appear, then turn and finish baking.

IT'S COFFEE PARTY TIME

Bake up something special—a fragrant, festive coffee cake—put on the coffee pot and you're ready to offer hospitality in the friendliest way.

Cherry-Raisin Coffee Cake
(See picture, p. 66)
Rich and spicy-sweet.

Heat oven to 400° (mod. hot). Make Coffee Cake batter from Basic Recipe (p. 12) except—spread batter in a greased 9x9x2" sq. pan. Sprinkle with a mixture of ¼ cup brown sugar (packed), ½ cup raisins and ¼ tsp. cinnamon. Spoon ⅔ cup cherry jam over top. Bake *20 to 25 min.* While warm, frost with Easy Creamy Icing (p. 58). Serve warm.

Peanut Butter and Jam Coffee Cake

Children will love this for an after-school snack.

   2 cups Bisquick
   ¼ cup sugar
   ¼ cup creamy peanut butter
   ¾ cup milk
   1 egg
   ½ cup orange marmalade or raspberry jam

Heat oven to 400° (mod. hot). Grease a 9x1½" round layer pan. Mix Bisquick and sugar. Cut in peanut butter. Stir in milk and egg; beat 30 seconds. Pour into prepared pan. Spoon marmalade thinly over top. Bake *about 25 min.*, or until nicely browned. Immediately frost with Easy Creamy Icing (p. 58). Serve warm.

Banana Coffee Cake
Moist and delicious.

Heat oven to 400° (mod. hot). Blend 2 tbsp. sugar, 1 egg, 1 cup mashed fully ripe bananas and 2 cups Bisquick. Beat vigorously 30 seconds. Spread into greased 8x8x2" sq. or 9x 1½" round layer pan. Blend 2 tsp. cinnamon, ¼ cup sugar, 2 tbsp. Bisquick and 2 tbsp. hard butter with a fork until crumbly. Sprinkle on top of batter. Bake *20 to 25 min.*

Chocolate Swirl Coffee Cake

   ⅓ cup flaked coconut
   ¼ cup chopped nuts
   ¼ cup sugar
   1 tbsp. butter, melted
   Richer Coffee Cake batter
   ⅓ cup semi-sweet chocolate pieces, melted

Heat oven to 400° (mod. hot). Mix coconut, nuts, sugar and butter; set aside. Grease an 8x8x2" sq. pan. Make Richer Coffee Cake batter from Basic Recipe (p. 12). Pour into prepared pan. Spoon melted chocolate over top; run a knife back and forth through batter to marble it. Sprinkle coconut mixture evenly over top. Bake *25 to 30 min.* Cut in squares and serve warm.

COFFEE TIME SHORTCAKES

refreshing, original and beautiful to behold!

Shortcake Kolaches
(See picture, p. 86)
Rich and quick to make with any jam or jelly.

Heat oven to 425° (hot). Make Shortcake dough from Basic Recipe (p. 10). Roll ½″ thick. Cut out six 3″ shortcakes. Dip fingers in flour and press a deep indentation (about 2″ across) in center of each shortcake; fill with a heaping tablespoonful of your favorite jam. Bake *about 10 min.*, or until lightly browned. Serve warm with whipped cream, commercial sour cream or cream.

Note: Be sure to make a deep indentation and do not let filling spill over sides.

Shortcake Kolaches with Prunes: Follow recipe (above) except—substitute Prune Filling (below) for jam.

Prune Filling: Simmer ½ lb. (a little over 1 cup) prunes in water to cover for 30 min., or until tender. Drain; pit; finely chop. Add ¼ tsp. allspice, ¼ cup sugar, grated rind of 1 lemon and 1 tbsp. lemon juice. Cool.

Strawberry Pineapple Shortcake

Heat oven to 425° (hot). Make Shortcake dough from Basic Recipe (p. 10). Roll ¼″ thick. Cut into sixteen 3″ rounds. Arrange 8 rounds on ungreased baking sheet; top each with a well drained pineapple slice. Fill center with brown sugar and top each with another round. Bake *10 to 15 min.*, or until lightly browned. Serve warm with sweetened strawberries and whipped cream.

Peach or Strawberry Shortcake Parisian

Shortcake "on the square" with brown sugar and sour cream.

Heat oven to 450° (hot). Make Shortcake dough from Basic Recipe (p. 10). Roll dough into two 8″ squares. Fit one piece into an 8x8x2″ pan. Dot with butter and sprinkle with ¼ cup brown sugar. Cover with other square. Bake *about 20 min.*, or until browned. Cut into squares. Serve warm with commercial sour cream and sweetened fruit.

MAGIC "QUICKIES"

for spur-of-the-moment coffee parties . . .

Cinnamon Thins

Crisp, spicy little discs sprinkled with nuts.

Heat oven to 450° (hot). Make Shortcake dough from Basic Recipe (p. 10). Form dough into 40 small balls (1″ across). Mix 1⅓ cups sugar and 3 tsp. cinnamon. Spread sugar mixture thickly on waxed paper. Coat each ball in mixture; then roll with rolling pin in oval shape; turn over several times and roll each time until they are thoroughly sugar coated and paper thin. Sprinkle each with ½ tsp. finely chopped nuts, pressing in lightly with rolling pin. Place on well greased baking sheet. Bake *4 to 5 min.*, until rich brown and crisp. Remove immediately from baking sheet. *Makes 40.*

Spicy Sticks

Heat oven to 450° (hot). Make Shortcake dough from Basic Recipe (p. 10)—except add ½ tsp. nutmeg, cinnamon or cardamom. Turn out on lightly greased baking sheet. With floured fingers, shape into a 12x8″ rectangle. Brush with milk. Sprinkle with mixture of 2 tbsp. sugar and ½ cup chopped pecans, pressing nuts gently into dough. Bake *about 15 min.*, or until lightly browned. Cut in half lengthwise; then in 2″ strips crosswise, *making 16 pieces.*

Chocolate Chip Velvet Crumb Cake

Chocolate mint wafers chopped in the batter.

Make Velvet Crumb Cake from Basic Recipe (p. 11)—except fold into batter ⅓ cup finely chopped chocolate mint wafers or rum-flavored chocolate wafers (about 13). Serve with whipped cream or your favorite topping.

Note: 1 tsp. rum flavoring may be used in place of vanilla when using rum wafers. In warm weather, chill chocolate mint wafers thoroughly before chopping them.

Graham Cracker Velvet Crumb Cake

Crunchy graham streusel topping.

Make Velvet Crumb Cake from Basic Recipe (p. 11) except add ⅔ cup finely crushed graham crackers (8) with the Bisquick. Sprinkle the warm baked cake with Graham Cracker Topping (below). Place about 3″ under broiler until mixture browns (2 to 3 min.). Do not burn!

Graham Cracker Topping: Mix ⅓ cup crushed graham crackers (4), ¼ cup Bisquick, ¼ cup sugar and 3 tbsp. butter or margarine thoroughly with fork or finger tips.

DESSERT PARTY DELICACIES

Butterscotch Meringue Cake
(See picture, p. 66)

A really elegant dessert in festive holiday dress.

    Velvet Crumb Cake
    1 egg white
    1 cup brown sugar (packed)
    ½ tsp. vanilla

Make Velvet Crumb Cake from Basic Recipe (p. 11). *Then heat oven to 400°* (hot). Beat egg white until frothy. Gradually beat in brown sugar and vanilla. Continue beating until very stiff. Spread over warm or cold cake. Seal to edges of pan. Bake *8 to 10 min.*, or until golden brown. Serve warm with Ruby Glow Sauce (below) spooned over top. *9 servings.*

Ruby Glow Sauce

    1 tbsp. cornstarch
    ¼ cup sugar
    ½ cup water
    ½ cup canned whole cranberry
      sauce

Mix cornstarch and sugar in saucepan. Stir in water and cranberry sauce. Bring to boil over direct heat, stirring constantly. Boil 1 min. If desired, add a few drops of red food coloring. Serve warm.

Note: For ease in serving, cut cake in serving-sized pieces while the meringue is still hot. Remove pieces from pan just before serving.

Velvet Fudge Cake

    1⅓ cups Bisquick
    ¾ cup sugar
    ⅓ cup cocoa
    3 tbsp. soft butter or
      shortening
    1 egg
    ¾ cup milk
    1 tsp. vanilla

Heat oven to 350° (mod.). Grease and flour a sq. pan, 8x8x2″. Mix Bisquick, sugar and cocoa. Add butter, egg and ¼ cup of milk. Beat 1 min. with electric mixer at med. speed or vigorously by hand. Stir in gradually remaining milk and vanilla. Beat ½ min. Pour half of batter into prepared pan. Spread with half of Chocolate-Coconut Icing (below). Pour remaining batter into pan. Bake *35 to 40 min.* Immediately spread with rest of icing. Serve warm.

Chocolate-Coconut Icing: Mix ½ cup (½ pkg.) semi-sweet chocolate pieces, melted, ⅓ cup water and 2 cups finely chopped coconut.

DECORATIVE UPSIDE-DOWN CAKES

Bake these just at party time . . . let their inviting aroma greet your arriving guests. Serve warm in tender, luscious squares.

Velvet Crumb Upside-Down Cake

So tender and rich—served warm from the oven, it makes an impromptu party of a casual call.

> 2 tbsp. butter or margarine
> ¼ cup brown sugar (packed)
> fresh or well drained canned fruit (suggestions below)
> Velvet Crumb Cake batter

Heat oven to 350° (mod.). Melt butter over low heat in bottom of 8x8x2″ or 9x1½″ round layer pan. Sprinkle with brown sugar. Arrange fruit over sugar mixture. Make Velvet Crumb Cake batter from Basic Recipe (p. 11). Pour over fruit in pan. Bake *40 to 45 min.*, or until toothpick inserted into center comes out clean. Invert at once on serving plate. Allow pan to remain over cake for a few minutes so sugar mixture will run down over the cake. Serve warm, plain or with whipped cream.

For Pineapple Upside-Down Cake:
Drain well 1 can (8½ oz.) pineapple slices. Arrange attractively in pan with cherries and nuts, if desired.

For Apricot Upside-Down Cake:
Arrange rows of fresh or well drained canned or stewed apricots over sugar mixture. A blanched almond looks attractive placed in center of each apricot.

Christmas Tree Upside-Down Cake

In a holiday mood? Here's a Christmas tree for every guest.

> 3 tbsp. butter or margarine
> ½ cup brown sugar (packed)
> 1 can (8½ oz.) pineapple slices (reserve juice)
> 1 maraschino cherry, cut into 8 slices
> 8 pecan halves
> Velvet Crumb Cake batter

Heat oven to 350° (mod.). Melt butter over low heat in bottom of 9x1½″ round layer pan. Sprinkle with brown sugar. Arrange fruit and nuts over sugar mixture (directions below). Make Velvet Crumb Cake batter from Basic Recipe (p. 11). Pour batter evenly over fruit in pan. Bake *40 to 45 min.* Invert at once on serving plate. Allow pan to remain over cake for a few minutes so sugar mixture will run down over cake. Serve warm, plain or with whipped cream.

To decorate: Add ½ tsp. green food coloring to pineapple juice. Cut each of 3 pineapple slices into eighths. Put half of these pieces (12) into green juice for a minute or two. Drain both pineapple and cherry slices well. To form tree trunks, arrange pecan halves at even intervals around edge of pan bottom. Make trees by forming triangles with 3 pineapple pieces each. Alternate green and yellow trees and top each with cherry slices.

REFRIGERATOR PIES

Fluffy, rich and elegant to make ahead of party time, garnish imaginatively and serve with a flair.

Lemon Mallow Short Pie

Baked Short Pie shell
32 marshmallows (½ lb.)
grated rind of 1 lemon
¼ cup lemon juice
½ cup water
1½ cups whipping cream,
  whipped

Make Short Pie shell from Basic Recipe (p. 15). Cool. In saucepan heat marshmallows, lemon juice, rind and water, stirring constantly, just until marshmallows are melted. Chill until partially set. Fold in whipped cream. Pile into Short Pie shell. Chill until set, at least 4 hr. Sprinkle with grated lemon rind.

Pineapple Mallow Short Pie

Baked Short Pie shell
32 marshmallows (½ lb.)
1 cup crushed pineapple,
  undrained
1 tbsp. lemon juice
1½ cups whipping cream,
  whipped
toasted almonds, chopped

Make Short Pie shell from Basic Recipe (p. 15). Cool. In saucepan heat marshmallows, pineapple and lemon juice, stirring constantly, just until marshmallows melt. Chill until partially set. Fold in whipped cream. Pile into Short Pie shell. Chill until set, about 4 hr. Sprinkle with chopped almonds.

Orange Mallow Short Pie

(See picture, p. 66)
Baked Short Pie shell
36 large marshmallows
¾ cup orange juice
2 tbsp. lemon juice
1 tbsp. grated orange rind
1½ cups whipping cream,
  whipped

Make Short Pie shell from Basic Recipe (p. 15). Cool. In saucepan heat marshmallows, juices and grated rind, stirring constantly, just until marshmallows melt. Chill until partially set. Fold in whipped cream. Pile into Short Pie shell. Chill 4 hr.

Chocolate Mousse Short Pie

Voilà! A simple-to-do version of a famous French dessert in rich, buttery crust.

Baked Short Pie shell
1 tbsp. unflavored gelatin
3 tbsp. water
1 cup chocolate syrup
2 cups whipping cream
½ cup sifted confectioners'
  sugar
¼ tsp. salt

Make Short Pie shell from Basic Recipe (p. 15). Cool. Soften gelatin in water and dissolve over hot water. Stir into chocolate syrup. Combine cream, confectioners' sugar and salt in chilled bowl and whip until stiff. Fold into chocolate mixture. Pour into Short Pie shell. Chill 3 to 4 hr.

Remove chilled pies from refrigerator 20 min. before serving.

PANCAKES AND WAFFLES

at their party-best.

Dessert Waffles Deluxe

These rich, cake-like waffles make an impressive dessert topped with fruit and whipped cream.

3 eggs, separated
1½ cups cream (20% butterfat)*
1 tsp. vanilla
2 cups Bisquick
1 tbsp. sugar

Blend egg yolks, cream and vanilla. Stir in Bisquick and sugar until smooth. Beat egg whites until soft peaks form; fold into Bisquick mixture. Bake in heated waffle iron. Serve at once. *Makes three 9″ waffles.*

*1½ cups cream (12% butterfat) may be used. With this cream, fold in 2 tbsp. melted butter or margarine after egg whites.

HOSTESS NOTE
You can "come out of the kitchen" at party time if you bake waffles several hours ahead. Just before serving, place them in a single layer on a baking sheet and reheat to crispness 4 min. in 400° oven, turning once.

Thin Pancakes with Cream Cheese and Pineapple Syrup

Delicate "crêpes" — a continental glamour dessert.

Make Thin Pancakes (below). Soften 2 pkg. (3 oz. each) cream cheese with ¼ cup cream. Spread about a tbsp. cheese mixture across one side of baked pancakes; roll up pancakes; place close together in shallow baking pan. These may be made, rolled and kept for a couple of hours. Just before serving, reheat 10 min. in 400° (mod. hot) oven. Serve 2 per person with warm Pineapple Syrup (below).

Thin Pancakes: Beat 2 eggs, 2 cups milk and 2 cups Bisquick with rotary beater until smooth. Lightly grease a 6 or 7″ round skillet. Spoon about 3 tbsp. batter at a time onto hot skillet. Tilt pan to coat bottom. Bake until bubbles appear. Loosen edges gently and turn to finish baking. Keep pancakes warm between towels until ready to serve.

Pineapple Syrup: Boil 2 cups sugar, 1 can (6 oz.) frozen pineapple juice concentrate, ½ cup butter and ¼ cup water together for 5 min. Store leftover syrup in refrigerator. It does thicken—reheat for serving.

TEA TABLE TRIUMPHS

Moist, deliciously rich fruit and nut breads make delightful little tea sandwiches for two, twenty or two hundred.

(See picture, p. 86)

For Holiday Tea Parties serve colorful Cardamom Cherry Nut Bread, Gum Drop Nut Bread and Cranberry Nut Bread, (p. 83).

Nut Bread

3 cups Bisquick
½ cup sugar
1 egg
1¼ cups milk
1½ cups chopped nuts

Heat oven to 350° (mod.). Mix first four ingredients. Beat vigorously 30 seconds. Stir in nuts. Pour into well greased loaf pan, 9x5x3″. Bake *45 to 50 min.*, or until toothpick inserted in center comes out clean. Cool before slicing.

Nut breads freeze very well for 2 to 3 months. Wrap in freezing wrap. Defrost in wrap at room temperature for 1½ to 2 hours before serving.

Little Nut Bread Loaves

Charming for small holiday gifts . . . unusual and fun for luncheon or dinner.

One recipe of Nut Bread will make 6 small loaves. Make Nut Bread (left)—except divide batter equally among 6 well greased miniature loaf pans, 4¾x2⅝x1½″. Bake at 350° (mod.) *about 35 min.*

Round Nut Breads Baked in Cans

Make Nut Bread (left)—except divide batter equally among 3 well greased no. 2 cans or 5 well greased soup cans, filling each can slightly more than half full. Bake at 350°, no. 2 cans *45 to 50 min.*, soup cans *about 40 min.*

Nut Bread Sandwiches: Slice nut bread very thin with sharp knife. Put slices together with a filling of softened butter or cream cheese, flavored if desired, and cut as sketched (below). OR serve open faced, cut into fancy shapes and spread with your favorite cheese.

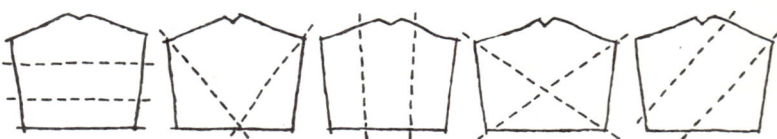

PARTY FRUIT AND NUT BREADS

Banana Nut Bread: Make Nut Bread (p. 82)—except use ¾ cup sugar and only ½ cup milk. Use only ¾ cup chopped nuts and add 1 cup mashed bananas (2 to 3 bananas). *Bake 55 to 60 min.*

Orange Nut Bread: Make Nut Bread (p. 82)—except use ¾ cup sugar and instead of milk, use orange juice plus 1 tbsp. grated orange rind. Use only ¾ cup chopped nuts. Bake *50 to 55 min.*

Poppy Seed Nut Bread:

Make Nut Bread (p. 82)—except add ¼ cup poppy seeds, grated rind of 1 lemon or 1 orange. Use only ¾ cup chopped nuts. Bake *45 to 50 min.*

Sesame Seed Loaf Bread:

Make Nut Bread (p. 82)—except add 1 pkg. (2½ oz.) sesame seeds, toasted, to the batter. Omit nuts. Bake *45 to 50 min.* To toast sesame seeds, see (p. 19).

Cardamom Cherry Nut

Bread: Make Nut Bread (p. 82)—except add ½ tsp. powdered cardamom and 1 cup candied cherries, cut up. Use only ¾ cup coarsely chopped walnuts or pecans. Bake *55 to 60 min.*

Gumdrop Nut Bread: Make Nut Bread (p. 82)—except add 1 cup assorted gumdrops, cut in pieces (omitting black ones). Bake *50 to 55 min.*

Note: For ease in cutting gumdrops, use kitchen shears dipped occasionally in water.

Cranberry-Orange Nut Bread

A "Merry Christmas" bread— colorful, tangy and rich— to give or serve at holiday time.

> ¾ cup sugar
> 1 egg
> 1¼ cups orange juice
> 1 tbsp. grated orange rind
> 3 cups Bisquick
> ¾ cup chopped nuts
> 1 cup chopped cranberries
> (fresh or frozen, if frozen
> do not thaw)

Heat oven to 350° (mod.). Mix sugar, egg, orange juice, rind and Bisquick. Beat vigorously 30 seconds. Batter may still be lumpy. Stir in nuts and cranberries. Pour into well greased loaf pan, 9x5x3". Bake *55 to 60 min.*, until toothpick inserted into center comes out clean. Crack in top is typical. Remove from pan. Cool before slicing.

TEA PARTY COOKIES

rich, pretty and unusual sweets for the tea table.

Fudge Squares

(See picture, p. 86)

    2 sq. unsweetened chocolate
    (2 oz.)
    ¼ cup butter or margarine
    1 cup sugar
    2 eggs
    1¼ cups Bisquick
    ½ cup chopped nuts

Heat oven to 350° (mod.). Melt chocolate and butter together. Mix in sugar, eggs, Bisquick and nuts. Spread in greased square pan, 8x8x2" or 9x9x2". Bake *30 to 35 min. Do not over bake.* Cool and cover with Topping (below). Cut into 1" squares.

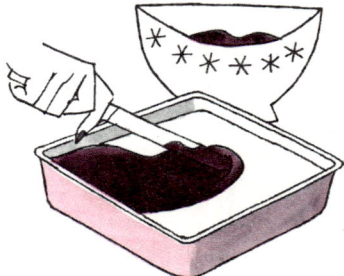

Topping: Cream together ¼ cup butter, 1 tbsp. milk, 2 cups sifted confectioners' sugar and 1 tsp. vanilla. Spread over Fudge Squares. Melt 1½ sq. unsweetened chocolate (1½ oz.); spread evenly over top.

Mincemeat Cooky Bars

They begin like biscuits—turn into delicious little cookies.

    2½ cups Bisquick
    1 cup sugar
    1 egg
    3 tbsp. butter or margarine
    1½ cups prepared mincemeat

Heat oven to 375° (quick mod.). Mix thoroughly all ingredients except mincemeat. Pat half of dough into a greased oblong pan, 13x9½x2", to within ½" of each edge. Spread with mincemeat. Pat out other half of dough on waxed paper to same size. Invert over mincemeat; pull off waxed paper. Bake *30 min.* If desired, frost with Easy Creamy Icing (p.58). Cut while slightly warm into 2¼x 1½" bars.

Date Squares

    ¼ cup butter or margarine
    ¾ cup sugar
    1 egg
    1⅓ cups Bisquick
    ½ cup chopped nuts
    1 cup cut-up dates

Heat oven to 350° (mod.). Grease an 8x8x2" sq. pan. Mix thoroughly butter, sugar and egg. Stir in Bisquick, nuts and dates. Spread in prepared pan; bake *25 min.* Cool about 1 hr. Cut into squares. Roll in confectioners' sugar.

Fruit Chews
Chockful of colorful fruits.

   1 cup sugar
   ¼ cup soft butter or margarine
   2 eggs
   1 cup Bisquick
   1 cup chopped walnuts
   1 cup chopped dates
   1 jar (4 oz.) maraschino cherries, drained and chopped

Heat oven to 350° (mod.). Mix sugar, butter and eggs well. Stir in Bisquick. Fold in nuts, dates and cherries. Spread in well greased oblong pan, 13x9½x2". Bake *30 min.* Cool in pan for 10 min. Loosen edges with spatula and cut in 2¼x1½" bars. Remove from pan carefully because cookies are delicate when warm. Sprinkle with or roll in confectioners' sugar. *Makes 32 bars.*

Candy Dandies
Heat oven to 375° (quick mod.). Mix ¼ cup butter, ¾ cup brown sugar (packed) and 1 egg; stir in 1⅓ cups Bisquick, ½ cup chopped nuts and 1 cut up chocolate-covered coconut candy bar. Drop by teaspoonfuls 2" apart on greased baking sheet. Bake *10 min.* or until lightly browned. *Makes 3 to 4 doz.*

Peek-A-Boo Filled Cookies
Rich with dates and crunchy nuts.

   Date Filling (below)
   ½ cup soft butter or margarine
   1¼ cups brown sugar (packed)
   2 eggs
   1 tsp. vanilla
   3 cups Bisquick

Prepare Date Filling. Heat oven to 375° (quick mod.). Blend butter and brown sugar. Stir in eggs, vanilla and Bisquick; blend well. Drop by teaspoonfuls on ungreased baking sheet; spread slightly. Top with Date Filling. Drop a smaller amount of dough (than used for bottom of cooky) on top of date filling. Bake *10 to 12 min.*, or until lightly browned. *Makes about 4 doz. cookies.*

Date Filling
   1½ cups dates, chopped
   ½ cup sugar
   ½ cup water
   ¼ cup chopped nuts

Cook dates, sugar and water slowly, stirring constantly, until mixture thickens. Add nuts; cool.

SUNDOWN SPECIALTIES

*For easy and fun party-giving, entertain at Open House
or before dinner with these "make-ahead" appetizers.*

Cheese Snacks

*Tender-light, fluffy little balls
with zesty cheese flavor. Parsley-
speckled, delicately brown.*

    1 cup Bisquick
    ½ cup grated sharp yellow
       cheese
    2 tbsp. mayonnaise
    ⅓ cup milk
    ½ cup chopped parsley or chives
    1 tbsp. grated onion

Heat oven to 450° (hot). Blend Bisquick, cheese, mayonnaise and milk
thoroughly with fork. Shape into
½″ balls. Roll in mixture of parsley
and onion. Bake on greased baking
sheet *8 to 10 min. Makes about 30.*

Short Pie Teasers

A surprise in every bite!

Make Short Pie dough from Basic
Recipe (p. 15). Shape a small amount
of Short Pie dough around button
mushrooms or stuffed green olives,
well drained, cocktail wieners, cocktail sausage, or an assortment of
these. Dip tops in celery seeds or
poppy seeds. Place on ungreased
baking sheet. When ready to serve,
bake *8 to 10 min.* in 450° oven (hot).
Makes 3 doz.

Hot Seafood Appetizers

(See picture, p. 86)
*Miniature party biscuits—each a
bite of flavorful seafood and
flaky hot biscuit.*

Heat oven to 450° (hot). Make Biscuit dough from Basic Recipe (p. 7).
Roll a little more than ¼″ thick on
lightly floured cloth-covered board.
Cut into tiny biscuits about 1″ in
diameter. Place on baking sheet.
Bake *6 to 8 min.* Immediately split
each biscuit. Spread with a seafood
mixture (below); sprinkle with
grated sharp cheese. Replace tops.
Return to oven to heat. Serve piping
hot. *Makes about 60 tiny biscuits.*
Note: For pretty pink appetizers with
a slight tomato flavor, use tomato
juice in place of milk when making
the biscuit dough.

Shrimp Spread: Mix together ½
cup flaked cooked shrimp (5 oz.
can), 1 tbsp. chopped pimiento, 1
tbsp. lemon juice, 3 tbsp. mayonnaise and salt and pepper to taste.

Crabmeat Spread: Use crabmeat in
place of shrimp in the above recipe.

Make biscuits and fillings early in
the day. Fill and heat as needed.

*Left table: Hot Appetizers, pp. 87, 88, 90.
Right table: Dessert Snacks, pp. 84, 91.
Center table: Kolaches, p. 76 and Nut Breads, pp. 82, 83.*

PIPING HOT, HEARTY SNACKS

Tuna Biscuit Squares
Tangy, tasty finger food.

    Biscuit dough
    1 can (7 oz.) tuna, drained and
       flaked
    ¼ cup sweet pickle relish
    ½ tsp. salt
    1 tbsp. prepared mustard, if
       desired
    3 tbsp. mayonnaise

Heat oven to 450° (hot). Make Biscuit dough from Basic Recipe (p. 7). Divide in half. Pat half in 9″ sq. on greased baking sheet. Mix other ingredients and spread on dough. Pat out other half of dough into a 9″ sq. and place over filling. Bake *10 to 12 min.* Cut in squares and serve as snacks.

Ham Biscuit Squares: Make Tuna Biscuit Squares (above)—except fill with mixture of ½ lb. ground cooked ham (2 cups), ¼ to ½ tsp. prepared mustard and 3 tbsp. mayonnaise.

Wiener Boats
(See picture, p. 86)
Easy to make—fun to eat.

Heat oven to 400° (mod. hot). Make Shortcake dough from Basic Recipe (p. 10). Roll into a rectangle, 15x6″. Cut into ten 3″ squares. Place ½ of a wiener, cut crosswise, a piece of cheese, same size, and 1 tsp. chili sauce or catsup on each square. Seal each end to form a boat. Stick toothpicks through sides to hold sides of boat to wiener. Bake on baking sheet *15 to 20 min.*

Broiled Sandwich Deluxe
Tomato, ham and cheese.

Heat oven to 450° (hot). Make Biscuit dough as directed in Basic Recipe (p. 7)—except do not knead. Spread on greased baking sheet to make oblong, 10x8″. Spread top with soft butter or margarine. Bake *10 to 12 min.*

Slice 1 large tomato into 8 slices; season. Spread 8 boiled ham slices with prepared mustard. Slice 8 strips of cheese large enough to cover tomato and ham. Cut baked bread into 8 pieces. Top each piece with tomato, ham and cheese. Put under broiler until cheese melts. Serve immediately. *6 to 8 servings.*

Other Interesting
Variations: Add 2 tbsp. minced onion or chives or other desired herbs or seasonings to Biscuit dough.

• Use 1 can (6½ oz.) tuna, moistened with mayonnaise in place of ham and mustard.

• Use cooked bacon strips in place of ham and mustard.

• Use sliced turkey or chicken in place of ham and mustard.

PIZZA . . .

Yeast Pizza Dough

¾ cup warm water (not hot—
   110 to 115°)
1 pkg. active dry yeast
2½ cups Bisquick

Dissolve yeast in warm water. Add Bisquick and beat vigorously. Turn dough onto well floured surface. Knead until smooth, about 20 times. Divide dough into 4 pieces. Roll each piece paper-thin into a circle, about 10″ in diameter. Place on ungreased baking sheets or in shallow pie pans. Finish with topping (right).

Note: Allowing pizza dough "to rest" a few minutes after kneading will aid in rolling it to paper-thinness. Be careful not to tear dough.

Pizza Italiano Topping

¾ cup chopped onion
1 clove garlic, chopped
2 cups tomato sauce
about 1 cup chopped salami
   OR cooked Italian sausage
   OR 2 cans anchovies,
   chopped
salt and pepper to taste
2½ cups grated mozzarella
   cheese OR 2 pkg. (6 oz. each)
   sliced mozzarella cheese (cut
   into thin strips)
oregano

Mix onion, garlic, tomato sauce, salami, salt and pepper; spread on dough. Sprinkle grated cheese over all or lay cheese strips on top. Sprinkle with oregano to desired taste. *Heat oven to 425°* (hot). Bake *15 to 20 min.*, until crust is brown and filling hot and bubbly. Serve immediately. To eat, cut into pie-shaped wedges. Fold each wedge over and eat with fingers. Serve with tossed green salad and coffee.

. . . And More Pizza!

Hamburger Pizza: Make Pizza (above)—except use 1 lb. cooked ground beef and ½ cup chopped green pepper in place of salami, Italian sausage or anchovies.

Pepperoni Pizza: Make Pizza (above)—except use 1 cup sliced pepperoni in place of salami, Italian sausage or anchovies.

Tuna Pizza: Make Pizza (above)—except use 1 can (6½ or 9 oz.) tuna, drained and flaked, and 1 can (8 oz.) mushrooms, sliced and sautéed in butter or margarine, in place of salami, etc. Omit the garlic.

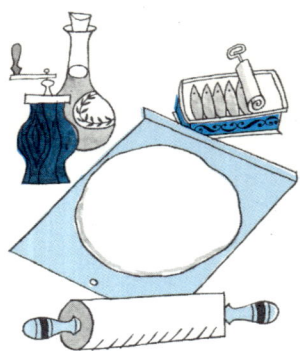

Quick Pizza Pie

Easy, crusty-shelled pizza made from biscuit dough.

2 cups Bisquick
½ cup water
½ cup grated Parmesan cheese
1½ to 2 cups well drained cooked tomatoes, cut in small pieces
½ lb. nippy cheese, cut in small pieces
1 can (2 oz.) anchovies, chopped, OR 1 can sardines OR 1 cup chopped salami
dash of coarsely ground pepper
2 tbsp. vegetable oil
½ medium onion, grated

Heat oven to 425° (hot). Mix Bisquick and water. Knead about 1 min. on lightly floured surface. Roll out ¼″ thick into a circle. Place on baking sheet. Pinch edge of dough to make a slight rim. Place other ingredients on dough in order listed above. Bake *20 to 25 min.*

Bits of Pizza: For individual pizzas, cut dough into 3″ squares. Pinch to build up edges of squares. Fill with desired filling or have all ingredients available for guests to make their own. Bake at *425°* for *15 to 20 min.* (See picture, p. 86)

PIZZA PARTY FUN

• Serve pizza for supper with salad.

• Invite teen-agers to concoct their own creative pizza fillings from bowls of sliced ripe, green or stuffed olives, onions, Parmesan, mozzarella, Roman, Cheddar, Ricotto or dry cottage cheese, sliced mushrooms, anchovy fillets, shrimp, pepperoni, salami, bacon, ground beef, diced ham, luncheon meat or skinless sliced frankfurters.

• Add a relish platter of raw vegetables.

• Pour tall glasses of milk and top off the meal with fresh fruit.

Batter Franks

1 egg
½ cup milk
1 cup Bisquick
2 tbsp. yellow corn meal
¼ tsp. paprika
½ tsp. dry mustard
⅛ tsp. cayenne pepper
1 lb. frankfurters (8 to 10)

Heat deep fat to 375°. Blend egg and milk. Stir in dry ingredients. Dip frankfurters into batter. Fry until brown, 2 to 3 min. on each side. Drain on absorbent paper. Insert a wooden skewer in the end of each frankfurter for eating on a stick. Serve with catsup or a spicy sauce.

Bring frankfurters to room temperature to keep fat from cooling too quickly.

SWEET TOOTH SNACKS

"Plate 'n fork" refreshments to serve when you entertain for an evening of TV, cards or a club meeting.

Jam Dandies

Sweet-filled biscuit wedges with sugary-nut filling. Serve piping hot.

Heat oven to 400° (mod. hot). Make Biscuit dough from Basic Recipe (p. 7)—except add 2 tbsp. sugar. Divide dough in half. Pat or roll each half into an 8″ round. Place one round in an 8″ layer cake pan. Spread with ½ cup of your favorite jelly or jam. Cover with remaining round of dough. Sprinkle top with ¼ cup *each* sugar and chopped nuts. Cut into 8 pie-shaped wedges. Bake *20 to 25 min.* Serve warm.

Velvet Crumb Cake with Broiled Orange Glaze
(See picture, p. 86)
Pure luxury eating.

Make Velvet Crumb Cake from Basic Recipe (p. 11)—except use brown sugar (packed) instead of granulated sugar. Bake *35 to 40 min.* While cake is warm, cover with Orange Glaze (below). Place about 3″ under broiler until mixture bubbles and browns (2 to 3 min.). Do not burn!

Orange Glaze: Mix 2 tbsp. soft butter, 3 tbsp. Bisquick, ¼ tsp. cinnamon, 2 tbsp. grated orange rind and ¼ cup brown sugar (packed).

Strawberry Minute Short Pie

This cooky-like crust holds a delicate, fruit-gelatin filling.

Make Short Pie shell from Basic Recipe (p. 15). Cool. Dissolve 1 pkg. *strawberry-flavored gelatin in 1 cup hot water. Add 1 pkg. *frozen strawberries (unthawed). Break up berries with a fork. As berries thaw the gelatin thickens. When filling is slightly thickened, pour into baked Short Pie shell. Chill until completely set. Remove from refrigerator 20 min. before serving. Garnish with sweetened whipped cream.

*Raspberry-flavored gelatin and frozen raspberries may be used.

Velvet Crumb Peach Shortcake

So tender and elegant — a beautiful ending to dinner or an evening.

Make Velvet Crumb Cake from Basic Recipe (p. 11). After baking, cut cake into 6 to 9 pieces while warm. Spoon sweetened sliced peaches over top. Pieces of cake may be split and served with peaches between and on top. Serve warm with whipped cream.

BAKING BIGGER BATCHES

Biscuits by the Dozens

60 Medium Biscuits—30 servings.
   10 cups Bisquick (40-oz. pkg.
      or two 20-oz. pkg.)
   3⅓ cups milk
100 Medium Biscuits—50 servings.
   15 cups Bisquick (60-oz. pkg.)
   5 cups milk

Follow directions in Basic Biscuit Recipe (p. 7).

Pancake Supper Party

Just for an evening, turn your house into a Pancake House. Borrow an extra griddle or two; bake up the cakes and serve—hot, light and tender—with an array of special syrups (p. 22).

60 Pancakes—15 servings.
   10 cups Bisquick (40-oz. pkg.
      or two 20-oz. pkg.)
   8⅓ cups milk
   5 eggs
100 Pancakes—25 servings.
   15 cups Bisquick (60-oz. pkg.)
   3 qt. milk
   7 eggs

Follow directions in Basic Pancake Recipe (p. 8).

Golden Ham Bake

A beautiful and delicious lunch or dinner dish—golden cheese biscuits on creamed ham! So easy to make for a crowd.

   ½ cup chopped onion
   ¾ cup chopped green pepper
   ¾ cup butter or margarine
   1 cup Bisquick
   6 cups milk
   3 cans (10½ oz. each) cream of
      mushroom soup
   6 to 7 cups diced cooked ham
   3 tbsp. lemon juice
   Cheese Biscuits (below)

Heat oven to 450° (hot). Sauté onion and green pepper in butter. Blend in Bisquick. Cook over low heat, stirring until mixture is bubbly. Remove from heat. Stir in milk and soup. Bring to boil over low heat, stirring constantly. Boil 1 min. Remove from heat. Stir in ham and lemon juice. Pour into 2 greased baking dishes, 13x9½x2″. Place in oven to heat while making Cheese Biscuits. Quickly place biscuits on hot mixture. Bake immediately *15 to 20 min. Makes 18 to 24 servings.*

Cheese Biscuits: Add 1 cup milk, 2¼ cups grated sharp cheese, 3 tbsp. chopped pimiento to 3 cups Bisquick. Stir with fork all at once to a soft dough. Beat vigorously 20 strokes, until stiff and slightly sticky. Divide in half. Roll out ¼″ thick. Cut about 30 biscuits with floured doughnut cutter, removing centers; place on ham. Use the centers to fill edges and corners of baking dish. Bake leftover biscuits on baking sheet *10 to 12 min.*

CAKES FOR A CROWD

The happy ending to a perfect party—this delectable, delicate cake with broiled topping is easy to bake and to serve.

Velvet Crumb Cakes

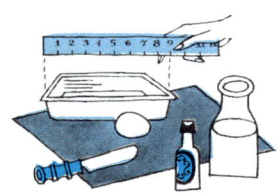

9" Square Cake

2 cups Bisquick
1 cup plus 2 tbsp. sugar
¼ cup soft butter or shortening
1 egg
1¼ cups milk
1½ tsp. vanilla

Heat oven to 350° (mod.). Grease and flour a 9x9x2" sq. pan. Mix Bisquick and sugar; add shortening, egg and ½ cup of the milk. Beat 1½ min. with electric mixer at medium speed or vigorously by hand. Gradually stir in the remaining milk and vanilla, and beat ½ min. more. Pour into prepared pan. Bake *40 to 45 min.* Cover with Broiled Topping (below) while warm. *Makes sixteen 2" squares.*

Broiled Topping: Mix ¼ cup soft butter, ½ cup brown sugar (packed), 3 tbsp. cream, ⅔ cup Wheaties or coconut and ⅓ cup chopped nuts. Spread on warm cake. Place about 3" under broiler until nicely browned (2 to 3 min.). Do not burn!

13x9½" Oblong Cake

2⅔ cups Bisquick
1½ cups sugar
6 tbsp. soft butter or
  shortening
2 eggs
1½ cups milk
2 tsp. vanilla

Follow mixing directions (left). Bake in 13x9½x2" oblong pan *35 to 40 min.* Cover with Broiled Topping (below) while warm. *Makes twenty-four 2" squares.*

Broiled Topping: Mix ⅓ cup soft butter, ⅔ cup brown sugar (packed), ¼ cup cream, 1 cup Wheaties or coconut and ½ cup chopped nuts. Spread on warm cake. Place about 3" under broiler until nicely browned (2 to 3 min). Do not burn!

Coffee Cake for a Party

4 cups Bisquick
¼ cup sugar
2 eggs
1½ cups milk

Heat oven to 400° (mod. hot). Mix ingredients. Beat vigorously 45 seconds. Spread into greased 13x 9½x2" oblong pan. Sprinkle with mixture of ⅔ cup brown sugar (packed), ⅔ cup Bisquick, ½ cup cold butter or margarine and 1 tsp. cinnamon blended with fork until crumbly. Bake *25 to 30 min.* Makes twenty-four 2" squares.

OPEN AIR
COOKERY

"Five of us are going on a two week back packing trip in the High Sierras. We plan on using Bisquick to a large degree..."

A. B. Coleman
Lompoc, Calif.

"I thought you might like to know how very much we enjoyed our vacation at Cape Cod with Bisquick along... when the family went clamming, I even used our favorite ... to fry the clams*. I introduced Bisquick to our summer neighbors, too..."

Mrs. Anna Marra
West Haven, Conn.

Breading fresh-caught fish to fry, making skillet biscuits or stew and dumplings over an open fire—you can cook dozens of hearty meals in the open air. For the backyard grill, on the trail or at a cabin in the woods, Bisquick and these recipes will make outdoor cooking a joy.

*See page 100 for Crispy Fried Fish and Seafood.

ON THE BACKYARD GRILL

Appeteasers

Fun for guests—"do-it-yourself" hot biscuit appetizers made on the grill.

Make Biscuit dough from Basic Recipe (p. 7). Season with celery seed or other spices for added zest. With floured fingers, take small balls of dough, wrap around any one of the following: Vienna sausages, cocktail wieners, shrimp or stuffed olives. Arrange assorted on tray and cover with foil for about 1 hr. before guests arrive. Place appetizers on charcoal grill and keep turning with tongs until brown on outside, *10 to 20 min.*, depending on heat from fire. Serve with chili sauce.

Strawberry Shortcake In Foil

A "do-ahead" strawberry shortcake to reheat and serve outdoors.

Make 6 individual Shortcakes from Basic Recipe (p. 10). Cool. Split and butter lightly. Wrap individually in double thickness of heavy-duty aluminum foil. Reheat over an outdoor grill (after coals are well burned down). Heat on each side from *2 to 4 min.* Serve immediately. Open foil and shape into a plate with an edge. Place strawberries between layers and over top. Serve with cream.

Cheese Bread

1 egg
1½ cups milk
3¾ cups Bisquick
¾ cup grated natural sharp
  cheese, such as Cheddar

Heat oven to 350° (mod.). Beat egg; add milk and stir in Bisquick and cheese. Beat 30 seconds until well blended. Pour into well greased, waxed-paper lined loaf pan, 9x5x3". Bake *1 hr.* Let cool a few minutes. Slice ½" thick and serve. Or, cool thoroughly, wrap in waxed paper and refrigerate overnight. Slice thin. Also good toasted.

Garlic Cheese Bread in Foil:

Slice Cheese Bread (above). Spread slices generously with Garlic Butter: garlic salt, used sparingly, or grated fresh garlic added to 1 stick (½ cup) butter or margarine. Reassemble loaf; wrap in aluminum foil and place on charcoal grill until bread is heated *15 to 20 min.*

**CAUTION TO
OUTDOOR COOKS**

Actual cooking time over open fires—coal, wood or charcoal—may be either more or less than approximate times given, as the heat varies and cannot be accurately controlled.

"INDOOR-OUTDOOR" PARTY SNACKS

*Tempting hot meat and chicken treats to bake in the kitchen,
then whisk outdoors to serve as your guests arrive.*

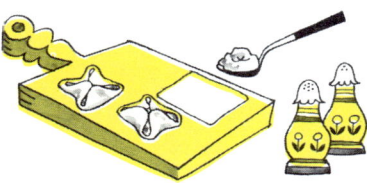

Chicken Puffs

*Transform leftover chicken into
patio party fare.*

Heat oven to 425° (hot). Mix ¾
cup cream with 2 cups Bisquick.
Turn dough over 2 or 3 times on
lightly floured surface. Roll out ¼"
thick into a rectangle, 20x8". Cut
into 10 squares, 4x4". Place a generous tbsp. of Chicken Filling (below)
on each square. Pull opposite corners up to center of square. Pinch
together to seal edges. Place sealed
side down in baking pan. Bake *20
to 25 min.* Serve hot. *Serves 10* as a
finger food.

Chicken Filling

1½ cups cooked chicken or
turkey
1 small onion, finely chopped
½ clove garlic, finely chopped
1 tbsp. butter or margarine
¾ cup commercial sour cream
¼ tsp. Worcestershire sauce
¼ tsp. salt
dash of pepper
¼ cup finely chopped stuffed
olives

Chop chicken finely. Brown onion
and garlic in butter. Mix with the
chicken and rest of ingredients.
Cook together over low heat for
about 5 min., stirring constantly.

Saucy Susans

Heat oven to 450° (hot). Make Biscuit dough from Basic Recipe (p. 7)
—except substitute tomato juice for
the milk. Roll dough ⅛" thick. Cut
into 1¼" rounds. Put each 2 rounds
together with a thin round of sharp
cheese between. Insert toothpick
through from top to bottom to hold
them together. Place close together
on baking sheet; sprinkle generously
with salt. Bake *8 to 10 min.*, until
lightly browned. Remove from baking sheet; serve hot. *Makes about 30.*

Pepperoni Squares

*Spicy sausage-biscuit squares to serve
as snack or main dish.*

2 cups Bisquick
2 hard-cooked eggs, chopped
½ stick pepperoni, chopped
1 tsp. oregano
2 tbsp. instant dried onion OR
½ cup chopped onion
⅛ tsp. pepper
⅔ cup milk

Heat oven to 450° (hot). Mix all
ingredients well. Spread in greased
9x9x2" sq. pan. Brush with soft butter or margarine. Bake *12 to 15
min.* Serve warm in squares with
mushroom, cheese or tomato sauce.

CROSS COUNTRY COOKING

Campfire Stew With Dumplings

Bring canned or homemade stew to a bubble in pot. Add ¼ cup plus 2 tbsp. milk or water to 1 cup Bisquick. Mix thoroughly. Drop dough by spoonfuls onto pieces of hot meat or vegetables. Cook *10 min.* uncovered and *10 min.* covered. *3 to 4 servings.*

Flapjacks
(See picture, p. 94)

Mix thoroughly 1⅔ cups milk or water and 2 cups Bisquick. Drop batter by spoonfuls onto lightly greased, hot pan. Turn when bubbles appear and the edges begin to dry. *Makes 12 to 14 flapjacks.*

Corn Flapjacks: add 1 cup drained whole kernel corn.

Corn Meal Flapjacks: use ½ cup corn meal in place of ½ cup Bisquick.

Blueberry Flapjacks: add 2 tbsp. sugar and gently fold in 1 cup blueberries.

Cheesy Pups
Hot dogs in a smoky bacon and cheese-flavored biscuit covering.

Make Biscuit dough from Basic Recipe (p. 7)—except add ½ cup grated sharp cheese to dough. Coat hands with Bisquick and pat dough around wiener making a thin covering. Smooth dough by patting with hands. Wrap one strip of uncooked bacon around dough, securing ends with toothpicks. Put on skewers or peeled sticks. Roast over hot coals. *Makes about 12.*

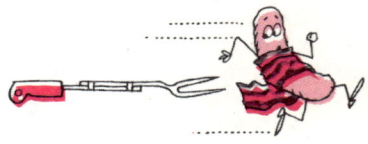

Onion Butter Biscuits
Charcoal baked, these are wonderful to serve with steak.

Melt ⅓ cup butter or margarine in metal pie pan on charcoal grill. Add 2 tbsp. dry onion soup mix. Spoon half of mixture into another pie pan. Make Biscuit dough from Basic Recipe (p. 7)—except add 2 tbsp. dry onion soup mix to Bisquick. Drop small biscuits into hot pie pan. Top with remaining butter mixture. Cover with other pie pan. Bake *8 to 10 min.* Turn each biscuit with spatula and bake *8 to 10 min.* longer.

Dough Balls

A trick for quickie hot breads. No extra equipment, no clean-up.

All you need: Several cups of Bisquick in plastic bag, milk or water, long, peeled sticks (diameter of little finger).

All you do: Set bag of Bisquick in upright position. Roll down sides to make a cuff. Take end of stick and push away Bisquick in center to make a small "well." Pour in about 1 tbsp. milk or water. Stir gently with stick until liquid picks up enough dough to form a soft ball around end of stick. Make ball about 1″ in diameter. It will expand during baking. Secure dough on end of stick by pressing gently with hand. Hold stick over coals, rotating slowly to bake ball and brown evenly, about *7 min.* Eat piping hot with butter, jam or jelly.

Twist Variation: Dust hands generously with Bisquick to prevent sticking. Remove ball of dough from stick before baking. Roll between hands into a strip about size of little finger, 4 or 5″ long. Wind strip of dough spirally around end of stick. Fasten securely by pinching ends. Bake as above. Slip off stick; fill hollow center with strip of cheese, cooked meat or spoon in jelly, jam or honey. Eat piping hot.

Fruit Dumplings

Heat to bubbling 1 can (1 lb. 13 oz.) fruit (3½ cups). Mix ¼ cup plus 2 tbsp. milk or water and 1 cup Bisquick thoroughly. Drop dough by spoonfuls onto hot fruit. Cook uncovered *10 min.* and about *10 min.* covered. *6 to 8 servings.*

Darn Goods

Crisp, doughnut-like puffs—delicious for breakfast on the trail.

    1 tsp. cinnamon
    2 tbsp. sugar
    vegetable oil
    ½ cup water
    1 cup Bisquick

Mix cinnamon and sugar in strong brown paper bag. Set aside. Heat oil (1½″ deep) in heavy skillet on top of grill over hot coals. Mix water and Bisquick. Dough should be stiff and sticky. When oil is hot, drop teaspoonfuls of dough into it; fry until rich golden brown and puffy. Drain on absorbent paper; shake in cinnamon-sugar mixture. *Makes about 12 puffs.*

Crispy Fried Fish

Turn the day's big catch into a fisherman's feast around the campfire. Bisquick makes an excellent crisp coating for fried fish or seafood.

For Fresh Fish: Coat all sides in Bisquick. Dip in sweet or sour milk or in buttermilk; roll again in Bisquick. Sauté in a small amount of fat until evenly browned.

For Seafood: Dip in slightly beaten egg; roll in Bisquick.

Skillet Biscuits

Melt ¼ cup butter in 9 or 10″ skillet. Sprinkle with onion salt, garlic salt and paprika. Make Biscuit dough from Basic Recipe (p. 7). Pat out ½″ thick and cut into 12 biscuits. Dip biscuits in skillet to coat with seasoned butter. Arrange in skillet; cover with heavy-duty aluminum foil, tucking ends underneath. Bake over grill *about 15 min.*, or until done. Invert to serve so crisp browned bottom side is up. Good with steak and also with stew or chili.

Dinner-In-A-Can

A tasty outdoor dinner cooked in a can. For "hobo" parties or out-in-the-woods camping trips.

    1 lb. ground beef
    2 carrots
    4 tomatoes
    1 can (1 lb.) whole kernel corn,
      drained
    ½ recipe·Dumpling dough

Season meat as desired and divide into 4 patties. Grease four 1-lb. coffee cans. Place a meat patty in bottom of each can. On top of meat, place 3 or 4 thin strips of carrot, 3 slices of tomato and ¼ of the corn. Dot with butter; season with salt and pepper. Cover each can securely with heavy-duty aluminum foil, molding outer edges firmly against sides of can. Place on grill; cook *20 to 30 min.* Make ½ recipe Dumplings from Basic Recipe (p. 14). Remove covers from cans; drop small spoonfuls of dough into each can. Sprinkle with minced parsley, chives, garlic, onion salt or other seasonings. Cover; cook *15 to 20 min.* longer. *4 servings.*

IN THE REFLECTOR OVEN

Hot breads baked by an open flame
Make modern ovens seem most tame.
Flavor and quality add to the zest
Of oven baking at its best.

Drop Biscuits

Mix ⅔ cup milk or water and 2 cups Bisquick thoroughly. Drop dough with spoon on greased baking surface. Bake *10 to 15 min.* in hot oven until brown. *Makes 16 small or 8 large biscuits.*

Blueberry Trail Biscuits

Make Drop Biscuits (above)—except add 2 tbsp. sugar and carefully fold in 1 cup blueberries.

Sweet Cinnamon Rolls

Make Drop Biscuits (above)—except drop a small spoonful at a time into a mixture of cinnamon and sugar. Roll each piece to coat surface. Place on greased baking surface. Bake *8 to 10 min.* in hot oven until brown. *Makes 24 small cinnamon rolls.*

Bannock (Pan Biscuit Bread)

Make Drop Biscuits (above)—except spread dough into a greased pan. Bake *20 to 25 min.* in hot oven until brown.

Main Dish Shortcakes

Bake Drop Biscuits (above)—except split and spread with butter, serving with creamed meat or seafood between halves and on top.

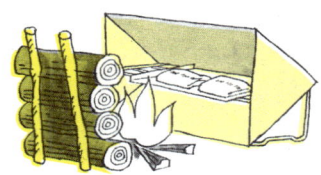

Meat Turnovers

Mix ½ cup milk or water, ¼ cup melted butter or margarine and 2 cups Bisquick thoroughly. Divide dough into 8 pieces. Place each portion on a piece of waxed paper which has been dusted generously with Bisquick. Pat out each to make a 5″ sq. Place a slice of cooked or canned meat on half of each square. Spread with chili sauce or pickle relish. Fold dough over meat and press edges together with tines of fork. Slit top of each turnover. Place on greased baking surface. Bake *15 to 20 min.* in hot oven until brown.

Crispy Corn Bread

Heat pan sizzling hot while mixing batter. Blend 1¼ cups Bisquick, ¾ cup corn meal and 2 tbsp. sugar. Stir in ¾ cup milk and 1 egg until blended. Turn batter into hot pan. Bake *about 15 min.* in hot oven until brown and crusty.

FROM
FARAWAY PLACES

"...we have 150 wonderful neighbors in the Ellice and Fiji Islanders ... I am the only white woman here ... Whenever there is a native feast, I take a huge, rich Bisquick cake and that is what they look forward to most."

Mrs. Frank Griffin, Canton Island
Phoenix Group, South Pacific

" On this tiny dot of a Dutch island off Venezuela in the Caribbean, I am using and appreciating your Bisquick."

Mrs. Edward Klock
Aruba, The Netherlands Antilles

Bisquick — international good will ambassador! Via air mail and slow boat, we receive letters and postcards from American homemakers all around the world. They tell us how much they depend on Bisquick to serve meals "just like back home" to their families and new foreign friends. Meanwhile, here in the United States we can enjoy traditional dishes of other lands, made the modern, easy way with Bisquick.

Danish Aebleskiver with Lingonberry Jam, p. 108.

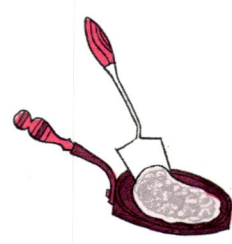

Swedish Dessert Pancakes

Scandinavian plättar, like the French crêpes, are tender, light and rich.

1¼ cups Bisquick
2 cups milk
3 eggs
¼ cup butter or margarine, melted

Beat all ingredients with rotary beater until blended. Lightly grease a 6 or 7″ skillet. Heat until a few drops of water sprinkled on it dance around before evaporating. Pour about 3 tbsp. batter into skillet, rotating pan to cover entire bottom. Cook until small bubbles appear on surface of pancake. Loosen edges with a spatula; turn over gently and finish baking. Place pancakes on towel or absorbent paper; set in oven (low heat) to keep warm. Spread each cake with sugar, jam or applesauce. Roll up like a jelly roll. Serve warm. *Makes about 16 pancakes . . . allow 2 per serving.*

Strawberry Blintzes

Elegant, classic dessert of Middle Europe. Make ahead of party time; reheat to serve.

Thin Pancakes (below)
1 cup cottage cheese (small curd)
1 pkg. (3 oz.) cream cheese
1½ tbsp. grated lemon rind
3 tbsp. lemon juice
¼ cup sugar
1 pkg. (10 oz.) frozen strawberries, thawed
1 tbsp. lemon juice
¼ tsp. almond extract

Make Thin Pancakes. Heat oven to 400° (mod. hot). Mix cottage cheese, cream cheese, lemon rind, 3 tbsp. lemon juice and sugar; whip until creamy. Place ¼ cup filling on each pancake and roll up. Place rolled side down in an oblong pan, 13x9½x 2″. Just before serving, heat in oven for 10 min. Heat strawberries, 1 tbsp. lemon juice and almond extract. Spoon over pancakes. Serve immediately. *6 servings.*

Thin Pancakes: Beat 1 egg, 1 cup milk and 1 cup Bisquick with rotary beater until smooth. Bake six 5″ pancakes. Keep pancakes warm between towels until ready to serve.

Cheese Soufflé

From the French cuisine; high, light, airy—a glamorous party dish, easy enough for everyday.

¼ cup Bisquick
½ tsp. dry mustard
1 cup milk
1 cup grated cheese
3 egg yolks, slightly beaten
3 egg whites
¼ tsp. cream of tartar

Heat oven to 350° (mod.). Mix Bisquick and mustard in saucepan; add small amount of the milk to make a paste. Stir in rest of milk gradually. Bring to boil; boil 1 min., stirring constantly. Stir in cheese. Remove from heat; stir gradually into egg yolks. Beat egg whites and cream of tartar until stiff. Fold in cheese mixture. Pour into ungreased 1½-qt. baking dish. Set baking dish in pan of hot water (1″ deep). Bake *50 to 60 min.*, or until silver knife when inserted near center comes out clean. Serve with a Mushroom Sauce (p. 46). *4 to 6 servings.*

VARIATIONS

Salmon Soufflé: Follow Cheese Soufflé recipe (above)—except season with salt and pepper in place of mustard. Substitute 1 cup flaked salmon for the grated cheese.

Chicken Soufflé: Follow Cheese Soufflé recipe (above)—except season with salt and pepper in place of mustard. Substitute 1 cup cut-up cooked chicken for the grated cheese. Add 1 tbsp. lemon juice.

Piroshki

Like the popular Polish appetizer sold hot by vendors in the city streets.

1 cup chopped canned
    corned beef
1 small onion, chopped
¼ cup grated cheese
1 tbsp. butter or margarine
3 to 6 drops Tabasco
½ recipe Biscuit dough
1 egg, beaten

Heat oven to 450° (hot). Mix first 5 ingredients. Make ½ recipe Biscuit dough from Basic Recipe (p. 7). Roll into rectangle, 12x6″. Cut into 3″ squares. Place filling in center of each square. Fold sides up; pinch and seal to form a boat. Brush with egg. Bake *about 10 min.* Serve with catsup or chili sauce or a cream sauce. *Makes 8 boats.*

Waffle Club Rabbit

Modern adaptation of Welsh Rabbit, a dish invented by peasants of Wales when they were forbidden to hunt small game for food on the estates of the nobility.

Make Waffles from Basic Recipe (p. 9). Serve waffles (whole or sections) with a slice or more of fresh tomato arranged on each serving. Spoon Cheese Sauce (p.56) over waffles; top with strips of crisp bacon.

Chinese Almond Cookies

Rich little cookies to end a meal with fine Oriental simplicity.

2 cups Bisquick
½ cup sugar
¼ cup shortening
1 egg, slightly beaten
½ tsp. almond flavoring

Heat oven to 350° (mod.). Mix all ingredients to form a stiff dough. Knead on lightly floured cloth-covered board for 1 min. Roll scant tablespoonfuls of dough into balls. Place balls 2″ apart on greased baking sheet. Flatten to ¼″ thick; press an unblanched almond into center of each. Bake *about 15 min.*, or until delicately brown. Makes about *2½ doz.*

Josephines

Dainty, fancy party dessert—our Short Pie version of the French pastry, Napoleon.

Make Short Pie dough from Basic Recipe (p. 15)—except add ½ tsp. almond or vanilla flavoring. Pat dough into twelve 3x2″ oblongs. Bake *6 to 8 min.* Cool. Just before serving spread tops of half the oblongs with Easy Creamy Icing (p.58). Sprinkle with chopped nuts. Put oblongs together in pairs with chilled vanilla pudding between. *6 servings.*

Italian Bread Sticks

Do as the Romans do—serve these buttery bread sticks with spaghetti dishes, salads and soups.

¾ cup warm water (not hot—110 to 115°)
1 pkg. active dry yeast
2½ cups Bisquick
¼ cup butter, melted

Dissolve yeast in warm water. Mix in Bisquick. Beat vigorously. Turn dough onto surface well dusted with flour. Knead until smooth, about 20 times. Divide dough into 16 equal parts. Roll each piece between hands into pencil-like strips, 8″ long. Spread part of butter in 13x9½x2″ oblong pan. Put strips of dough in pan. Brush tops with rest of butter. Sprinkle with caraway seeds, poppy seeds, celery seeds, sesame seeds or garlic salt. Cover with cloth. Let rise in warm place (85°) until light, about 1 hr. (If kitchen is cool, place pans on a rack over a bowl of hot water and cover completely with a towel.) *Heat oven to 425° (hot).* Bake *15 min.*, until light golden brown. Turn oven off. Allow bread sticks to remain in oven 15 more min. to crisp.

TRADITIONAL IN THE BRITISH ISLES

Scotch Scones

Tea and scones—a Highland favorite. Make them some day when it's too warm to heat the oven. Bake on the griddle; serve in toasty wedges.

2¼ cups Bisquick
2 tbsp. sugar
⅔ cup cream
1 egg
½ cup currants, if desired

Mix all ingredients to make a soft dough. Roll or pat into 12x8″ rectangle on lightly floured board. Cut into 6 squares; cut each square into 2 triangles. Bake *10 min.* on ungreased electric grill or heavy skillet on medium setting; turn and bake *10 min. longer. Makes 12.*

Holiday Fruit Scones

A festive English bread—fluffy, tender and tangy with fruit.

2 cups Bisquick
½ cup raisins or currants
2 tbsp. sugar
1 tbsp. grated orange rind
⅔ cup milk

Heat oven to 425° (hot). Mix Bisquick, raisins, sugar and orange rind. Stir in milk. Toss dough onto lightly floured cloth-covered board. Roll out into a 9″ round. Brush top with milk and sprinkle with sugar. Cut into 12 wedges and place on ungreased baking sheet. Bake *about 10 min.* Serve hot. *Makes 12 scones.*

Irish Soda Bread

The pride of Ireland made an easy modern way. A caraway and raisin adaptation baked in a skillet. Inexpensive, quick and good.

1 cup Bisquick
¼ cup raisins
1 tsp. caraway seeds
¼ cup plus 2 tbsp. milk

Heat oven to 450° (hot). Mix all ingredients together. Pat into a well greased 6″ skillet or deep baking pan. Bake *about 12 min.* Cut into wedge-shaped pieces. Serve hot with butter. *4 to 6 servings.*

London Buns

Rich and fruity—like those beloved by generations of British schoolboys.

¼ cup sugar
1 egg
¾ cup milk
2 cups Bisquick
2 tbsp. vegetable oil or butter or margarine, melted
1 cup raisins or currants
½ cup candied fruit (3 oz.)

Heat oven to 400° (mod. hot). Blend all ingredients; beat vigorously for 30 seconds. Fill greased muffin cups ⅔ full. Bake *12 to 15 min.,* or until golden brown. Serve hot. *Makes 20 small or 15 medium muffins.*

Danish Aebleskiver
(See picture, p. 102)

Denmark's housewives make these egg-rich little pancake balls in special cast iron pans, turning them to brown with their steel knitting needles.

    2 cups Bisquick
    ¾ cup milk
    5 egg yolks, unbeaten
    5 egg whites, well beaten,
      but not dry

Beat Bisquick, milk and egg yolks with rotary beater until well blended. Fold in egg whites. Place small amount of butter or margarine in each cup of Danish cake pan. Heat pan slightly; fill ⅔ full of batter. Cook until bubbly. Turn carefully with metal skewer; finish baking on other side. Remove from pan onto paper towels. Sprinkle confectioners' sugar over top and serve with lingonberry jam. *Makes about 42.*

With Apple Centers: Fill each cup ⅔ full of batter, add ½ tsp. well drained apple mixture (2 med. pared and finely grated apples, 1 tbsp. sugar and ¼ tsp. cinnamon) and cover with very small amount of batter. Bake as above.

English Trifle
(Tipsy Cake)

From the homeland of Dickens and Thackeray comes this justly famous dessert—a custardy, chilled cake with winey fruit flavor.

Make Velvet Crumb Cake from Basic Recipe (p. 11). Cool. Cut into 16 pieces. Slice each piece in half horizontally; spread slices with raspberry jam. Arrange like sandwiches in 11x7x1½″ glass baking dish. Sprinkle with ⅓ cup sherry flavoring. Prepare 1 pkg. (3 oz.) vanilla pudding mix as directed on pkg.—except add ½ cup more milk. Cool. Pour over cake. Sprinkle with ⅛ cup toasted slivered almonds. Spread with ¾ cup whipping cream, whipped and sweetened. Chill in refrigerator 4 hours. Top with chopped candied cherries. Cut in squares to serve.

the End

INDEX